Bigger Books Mean Amping Up Reading Power

Lucy Calkins, Lauren Kolbeck, and Brianna Parlitsis

Photography by Peter Cunningham

Illustrations by Marjorie Martinelli

HEINEMANN ◆ PORTSMOUTH, NH

This book is dedicated my mom, Rosanne Lagana, who always believes in me. Thank you for your love and encouragement.—Lauren

This book is dedicated to George, who reminds me to dream big, work hard, and never stop learning.—Brianna

This book is dedicated to my coauthors, with deep appreciation for their wells of energy, wisdom, resolve, and friendship.—Lucy

Heinemann
361 Hanover Street
Portsmouth, NH 03801–3912
www.heinemann.com

Offices and agents throughout the world

© 2015 by Lucy Calkins, Lauren Kolbeck, and Brianna Parlitsis

All rights reserved. No part of this book may be reproduced in any form or by any electronic or mechanical means, including information storage and retrieval systems, without permission in writing from the publisher, except by a reviewer, who may quote brief passages in a review, with the exception of reproducible pages, which are identified by the *Units of Study for Teaching Reading* copyright line and can be photocopied for classroom use only.

"Dedicated to Teachers" is a trademark of Greenwood Publishing Group, Inc.

The authors and publisher wish to thank those who have generously given permission to reprint borrowed material:

Pinkalicious: School Rules! by Victoria Kann. HarperCollins, 2010. Used by permission of HarperCollins Publishers.

From *Owl Moon* by Jane Yolen, illustrated by John Schoenherr. Text copyright © 1987 by Jane Yolen. Illustrations copyright © 1987 by John Schoenherr. Used by permission of Philomel, an imprint of Penguin Young Readers Group, a division of Penguin Random House LLC and by permission of Curtis Brown, Ltd.

Houndsley and Catina. Text copyright © 2006 James Howe. Illustrations copyright © 2005 Marie-Louise Gay. Reproduced by permission of the publisher, Candlewick Press.

Happy Like Soccer. Text copyright © 2012 by Maribeth Boelts. Illustrations copyright © 2012 by Lauren Castillo. Reproduced by permission of the publisher, Candlewick Press.

From *The Leaving Morning,* by Angela Johnson. Copyright © 1992 by Angela Johnson. By permission of Orchard Books, an imprint of Scholastic Inc.

Credit lines continue on p. 136

Cataloging-in-Publication data is on file with the Library of Congress.

ISBN-13: 978-0-325-07709-3

Series editorial team: Anna Gratz Cockerille, Karen Kawaguchi, Tracy Wells, Felicia O'Brien, Debra Doorack, Jean Lawler, Marielle Palombo, and Sue Paro
Production: Elizabeth Valway, David Stirling, and Abigail Heim
Cover and interior designs: Jenny Jensen Greenleaf
Photography: Peter Cunningham
Illustrations: Marjorie Martinelli
Composition: Publishers' Design and Production Services, Inc.
Manufacturing: Steve Bernier

Printed in the United States of America on acid-free paper
19 18   PAH   5

Acknowledgments

THIS BOOK STANDS on the shoulders of work that the three of us and our colleagues have been doing for years. We didn't invent this unit sitting at our writing desks—it has, instead, emerged as a favorite after years of teaching, revising, reinventing, and improving. The unit bears the handprints of children in San Francisco, Palm Beach, New Haven, and Ireland. It's been burnished with the loving input of brilliant teachers who have taught bits of it: here a sequence of work on figurative language, there a bit of teaching on fluency. The unit includes the wisdom of Tim Rasinski, who has made us far smarter about fluency, and the laughter of Kathy Collins, who helps us keep our ears down low, listening to small voices.

Above all, the book is the result of the collaboration of more than 60 staff developers. Each Thursday, when the staff of the Teachers College Reading and Writing Project (TCRWP) gathers to study together, our colleagues challenge our thinking, and again and again, teaching ideas that begin as grains of sand get turned into jewels. Without the support of our colleagues, none of this would be possible. A special thanks to Shanna Schwartz, Christine Holley, Monique Knight, Rebecca Cronin, Natalie Louis, Celena Larkey, Lindsay Barton, Rachel Rothman, Katie Wears, Marjorie Martinelli, Liz Dunford Franco, and Lindsay Wilkes. We can't forget the past staff developers as well, from whose knowledge we continue to grow: Joe Yukish, Enid Martinez, Mary Ann Colbert, and Kristi Mraz.

Leadership is what guides us through, raises us up and keeps us going. Kathleen Tolan is an intellectual thought companion like none other, Laurie Pessah makes all of our work and all of our relationships with schools possible. Amanda Hartman is always there for all of us.

We thank the teachers who helped us with this book throughout the year. Without them the unit would not have that special second-grade hand stamp. Thanks to Jennifer Goldman, Lindsey Conley, Stephanie Matthewson, and Debra Spinelli.

Within our community, there are people who make magic happen every day. We couldn't imagine the writing process without the amazing support of Julia Mooney. Sara Johnson and Gillian Osswald have worked tirelessly to help us. We are so thankful for all of the support we received from Julie Steinberg. It was a sigh of relief to know she was by our side. We also thank Beth Moore for her wise contributions.

It takes a village to make a book, and we thank all of the staff at Heinemann, especially Abby Heim, the leader of the team. Abby worked day and night, holiday and weekend, to help pull off this project. If there was something that we needed, Abby figured out how to make it happen. Marielle Palombo, our editor, read and reread each word for content and clarity, and revised many. We are thankful for her ability to see things that we couldn't and to be sure that our three voices came together as one. Peter Cunningham's pictures bring teachers and children into the book, and David Stirling's work with those pictures creates a coherent story.

Thanks, one and all.
—Lauren, Brianna, and Lucy

Contents

Acknowledgments • iii

An Orientation to the Unit • vi

BEND I Reading with Fluency

1. Rehearsing Reading Voices • 2

In this session, you'll teach children that reading aloud can help their in-their-head reading voices.

2. Scooping Up Words into Phrases • 8

In this session, you'll teach children that readers scoop up words into phrases and notice punctuation so that their reading makes sense and sounds right.

3. Noticing Dialogue Tags • 14

In this session, you'll teach children that dialogue tags can help readers read dialogue with expression.

4. Using Meaning to Read Fluently • 21

In this session, you'll teach children that readers match their voices to the meaning of the text.

5. Reading at a Just-Right Pace • 27

In this session, you'll teach students that readers make sure they read at a pace that is not too fast and not too slow—one that allows them to understand what they are reading.

BEND II Understanding Literary Language

6. Recognizing Literary Language • 34

In this session, you'll teach children that readers pay attention to literary language—comparisons, invented words, figurative language—asking, "What might the author want me to see, to understand?"

7. Understanding Comparisons • 41

In this session, you'll teach children that when authors use comparisons, they are signaling that they want readers to combine their knowledge of both things being compared and how they're alike.

8. Noticing When Authors Play with Words • 49

In this session, you'll teach children that readers notice when authors use language in creative ways by playing around with words. Readers work to understand what the author is really saying.

9. Reading as a Writer—Focusing on Special Language • 55

In this session, you'll teach children that when readers notice special language in a book, they think about the writer's craft and the special meaning the author wants them to get from that language.

BEND III Meeting the Challenges of Longer Books

10. Setting Up Routines for Same-Book Partners • 62

In this session, you'll teach children that reading the same books as a partner can help readers talk, clarify, and ask questions to better understand the books they are reading.

11. Holding On to Stories Even When Books Are Long • 70

In this session, you'll teach children that, as books become longer and more complex, readers jot down notes on Post-its to keep track of the story and remember the important things that happen.

12. Staying on Track When Books Get Tricky • 77

In this session, you could teach students that when readers don't understand what's happening, they don't keep going. They use their fix-up strategies. They slow down, reread, and ask questions.

13. Using Writing to Solve Reading Problems • 80

In this session, you'll teach children that readers can invent ways to use writing to help them tackle confusing parts in their reading.

BEND IV Tackling Goals in the Company of Others

14. Self-Assessing and Setting Goals • 90

In this session, you'll teach children to self-assess their own reading in order to set goals. They work with a reading club to help each other reach those goals.

15. Organizing Goal Clubs • 97

In this session, you'll teach readers that reading clubs need to create their own clear plans to accomplish their goals.

16. Giving Feedback to Group Members • 103

In this session, you'll teach children to support each other's work by giving helpful feedback.

17. Celebration • 108

In this session, you could celebrate all that the class has learned. You'll revisit the big skills of the unit and invite students to become researchers, learning from each other and sharing what they have learned.

Read-Aloud and Shared Reading

Read-Aloud • 112

Shared Reading • 123

Registration instructions to access the digital resources that accompany this book may be found on p. xiv.

An Orientation to the Unit

LAUNCHING INTO A NEW UNIT often begins with new resolve and reflection. Since the beginning of second grade, you have watched your readers grow bigger and stronger. Now, they are ready to be challenged in new ways, tackling longer and harder books. Above all, at the start of this unit you will convey that your students are ready for new challenges, and that each child is responsible for deciding what specifically he or she needs to work on to grow as a reader. This unit focuses on these three aspects of reading: fluency, literary language, and tracking longer stories. We encourage you to bring your own new energy and resolve to this unit on building foundational skills so that the work feels interesting, fresh, and challenging—yet within your readers' grasp.

Throughout the unit, you will rally readers around the idea that research scientists have been studying second-grade readers, and those scientists have found some critically important things about their subjects. You say, at the start of the unit, "Readers, you know how there are scientists who study bees, and there are scientists who study hurricanes. Well, there are also scientists who study *reading*. These are professors of reading, and to study reading they go into classrooms just like ours, with their clipboards and their pens behind their ears, and they watch and listen to kids reading." You go on to say that these research scientists have found that second grade is a time for readers to experience an enormous growth spurt.

This is an important message to communicate because too often, second-graders get into a holding pattern. As expectations of third-graders sky rocket (rightly or wrongly—that's for another day), it has become especially important that second-graders maintain the growth curve that characterizes first grade.

This unit has four parts. Each of the first three bends is focused on an important foundational reading skill. In the last bend, students get a chance to solidify, practice, and build on the work of the first three bends. In the first bend, "Reading with Fluency," you and your students will revisit what it looks and sounds like to read books with a smooth, expressive voice. Children will have focused on this skill at the start of the year, but several months have passed since then and children have begun reading substantially harder books, so practicing fluency will be valuable. In the second bend, "Understanding Literary Language," children explore figurative language. As students move into more sophisticated texts, the language becomes more complex. For example, in *I Love My Hair*, by Natasha Anastasia Tarpley, the author writes, "I love my hair because it is thick as a forest, soft as cotton candy, and curly as a vine winding upward" or in *Stellaluna*, Janell Cannon writes, "Her baby wings were as limp and useless as wet paper."

In the third bend, you'll help students keep track of the storyline in longer books. There is a big jump in length between books in the H/I/J band of text complexity and books in the K/L levels. This bend will teach students strategies for keeping track of longer texts as children move towards them. Finally, in the fourth and final bend, "Tackling Goals in the Company of Other," children will choose one of three clubs: Fluency, Literary Language, and Keeping Track of Longer Books, and they will form a club in pursuit of that goal.

THE INTERSECTION OF READING DEVELOPMENT AND THIS UNIT

There are many important reading skills that help readers build the solid reading foundation they'll need as they round the bend toward chapter books. Determining importance is an important skill for teachers as well as kids, then, because it is tempting to race around, touching on a lot of skills. It is important to decide on priorities and to invest in supporting skills that you decide are especially important. In this unit, helping children develop fluency will be one of your priorities, as the focus of Bend I is on fluency.

Tim Rasinski refers to fluency as the bridge between phonics and comprehension. Fortunately, a solid body of evidence suggests that fluency can be taught and that effective instruction in fluency leads to overall improvements in reading. In this unit, you will support key components of fluency, teaching phrased reading and rereading, while also modeling fluent, expressive reading. You'll want to check your youngsters' paces—those who are reading between levels I and M should be reading approximately 70 words a minute, with high levels of comprehension. If some of your children are reading faster than that, check whether they are missing important details and losing pieces of the story. Some of your children will presumably be reading slower than 70 words per minute, and you'll probably find that these children have a harder time accumulating text. These readers will be able to tell you what's happening on the page they are reading but will be less skilled at talking about how this page fits with earlier pages in the book. There are lessons in Bend I that help students practice working at a just-right reading rate, which for many of your children probably means picking up the pace, and doing so in ways that improve comprehension.

In addition to work on fluency, this unit helps your students understand literary language. You are apt to notice your readers fly over phrases in texts like the one from *Stellaluna*: "Her baby wings were as limp and useless as wet paper." If you interrupt to ask the reader about that bit of figurative language, you're apt to find that they interpret it very literally. Are her wings out of paper? Bend II teaches students to read closely and to monitor for sense, so that when they reach passages like that one they take note, stopping to ponder over what the author may have wanted them to think and feel. This is important work because it involves nudging readers to push past literal interpretations toward more interpretive ones. When students understand the literary language in their texts, their comprehension deepens because they can begin to think about nuance, tone, mood, and about how something is done. Their appreciation of texts grows as well. How beautiful it is, when reading *Owl Moon* by Jane Yolen, to read when Yolen compares milk to snow: "The snow below it was whiter than the milk in a cereal bowl." Since Bend II immerses students in texts with rich language, it will also be a great support for all of your students as they work on growing their vocabularies, especially your English language learners. Mem Fox reminds us that when we flood our classrooms with rich children's literature, and particularly when we read it aloud, students' vocabularies will grow naturally.

At the same time, children are reading books that are longer, and there is no question but that as the books children read become longer and more complex, readers have new work to do. They need to hold on to a storyline that threads across larger terrain. Before, when most of their books were episodic, comprising a sequence of self-contained mini-chapters, such as one sees in Frog and Toad and Henry and Mudge books, children didn't need to keep as many characters, events, and places in play in their minds as they need to do now that their books are more apt to be composed of one longer story. Bend III teaches students to keep track of these longer texts. You will teach specific reading comprehension strategies in the minilessons, and you'll also need to help students use these comprehension strategies during independent reading time, where you will see the most growth. Nell Duke's research indicates that when students use comprehension strategies they become better readers. While this research doesn't shock any teacher, it is great confirmation that we are on the right track, by helping students to home in on comprehension while reading.

At these levels of text, readers benefit from doing some talking with a same-book partner or doing a quick stop-and-jot at the end of the chapter to think about, "What just happened? How does that go with the earlier part?" Asking children to capture what is happening in a part of the text on a Post-it® is a useful challenge because Post-its don't have too much space, so readers will need to summarize the chunk of text. Bend III introduces students to using Post-its to help them keep track of a story.

In the last bend, students work together in clubs to reach their goals. When students work in groups, they not only practice important skills, they also learn how to be supports for each other. A study from the Institute of Education at London University suggests that for students to truly benefit from a group-work structure teachers should act as "guides on the side" of the groups, rather than jumping in and taking over.

Finally, you'll notice that many of the conferring sections in this unit are also designed to support students in strengthening their problem-solving skills. There is a heavy emphasis on coaching conferences and guided reading groups, where you'll listen in attentively as students read and coach only as needed with quick, clear prompts. We know children learn best by doing. By coaching kids to problem solve efficiently, you'll also be helping them get the feel of this work in their bones, setting them up to keep on doing it with complete independence.

OVERVIEW

Bend I: Reading with Fluency

Establishing an engaging and motivating context in which to teach reading comprehension is one of the key tenets that Tim Shanahan et al. outline in their practice guide, *Improving Reading Comprehension in Kindergarten Through 3rd Grade*. You will launch this unit by engaging students and motivating them to learn from research scientists about reading. In the first session of the first bend, students discover that rereading—especially out loud—is the best way to change the voice inside their heads. And that voice is everything, you'll explain. Reading with a clear, smooth voice inside one's head is a key to reading better, stronger, longer, and with more understanding. You may begin your teaching by letting students know that it is not just second-graders who need to reread. You may say, "Did you know that there are high school kids who read one piece of writing—the *same* piece of writing—every single day for the first month of school? The reason teachers have them do this is because teachers know that being able to read one thing *really* well can change the reading voice in your head."

You will ask readers, "Have you ever spoken into one of those big conch shells you see at the beach? When you speak into those shells, you can hear your voice as if it's in an echo chamber. With your hands, can you make a conch shell in front of your mouth? I am going to really listen to my voice as I read this story. Do the same—hold your shell up to your mouth and listen to your own voice as you read. Let's read with our best reading voices."

You'll stress to students, "It's the power of *rereading*, over and over." To reinforce this message, you might recruit the class to join in a song, sung to the tune of the "The Wheels on the Bus."

Read parts of our books again and again,	The wheels on the bus go round and round
out loud and in our heads,	round and round
out loud and in our heads,	round and round
Read parts of our book again and again,	The wheels on the bus go round and round
to make our reading *smooooooth!*	all through the *townnnnnnn!*

Using this song, you'll remind students to scoop up phrases, helping them realize that they can make their reading voices just as smooth as their singing voices by reading in longer phrases. They can scoop up more words at a time by noticing the punctuation. Then, they can check that their reading sounds right. This session goes beyond helping students put words into phrases when reading, as it also shows them that they can monitor their own reading by listening closely to how they sound. If your students have difficulty reading in phrases, you could make cards or lists from Tim Rasinski's "Phrases and Short Sentences for Repeated Reading Practice" from his book *The Fluent Reader* (95–99).

Children will learn not only to pay attention to their own reading voices but also to listen to the voices of the characters, reading those voices the way the author intended. You'll help them know that when they are reading dialogue, it is important to read in such a way that the character's voice (and personality and mood) comes through. The dialogue tags help with this, when they are present. They sometimes help readers determine who is talking and also help readers know how the character sounds. This means that your children can improve their intonation when they notice the dialogue tags. You may introduce a game to the class to practice for a bit to warm up. You might announce, "I've written a few different lines of dialogue on each sentence strip. You'll read a line, and then I'll choose a tag to add on. That means, I'll decide *how* it should sound. Then, you'll have a turn to add a dialogue tag." You may show the students a line such as "We are going to the beach today." Then, you change the dialogue tag. The students read it differently each time. Try it with "they whined" at the end or "they cheered." This will help students to learn to use dialogue tags to read with more expression.

Tim Rasinski often says that fluency is the bridge between phonics and comprehension. In this bend, you'll teach students that to read a book—even in their heads—and to make it sound right, readers also have to consider what it's about. If they are telling a best friend bad news, their voice will sound differently than if they are telling that friend about winning first place in a contest. When they know what the text is about, they can show that with their voice.

As you begin your next reading workshop, you might model different tones of voice. You might say, "Come to the rug," in an unusually brash tone. Then you might say, "Good morning, readers" in a kind tone, and watch to see how the students' responses change. You might point out the way you changed your voice, saying, "Readers, did you see how I used two different voices there? When I wanted you to come quickly to the rug, I used an authoritative tone of voice. When you heard that tone, you immediately knew I meant business and came to the rug. Then, when I said 'Good morning,' I was using my usual kind, sweet voice, and you relaxed. I'm telling you this because readers need to study the way that authors indicate the appropriate tone of voice to use when reading a text."

As you provide closure to the bend, the final session ends with a focus on pace. You will teach students that the aim is not reading fast, but rather finding your just-right pace. You will show children what you mean by saying, "If you go too fast, your words/all/blur/together, and . . . if . . . you . . . go . . . too . . . slow, it's hard to make sense of the text. Readers learn to adjust their speed so it's just right." You might ask, "How many of you remember the story *Goldilocks and the Three Bears*? Remember how she kept testing different things out until she found what was just right for her? Her story makes me think of you and how, as second-graders, you are figuring out your just-right reading pace." This bend will cover the three P's of fluency: pace, phrasing, and most important, prosody. Rereading will be a thread that is woven throughout the bend to help students read more fluently.

Bend II: Understanding Literary Language

In the books that your children are starting to read now, the authors often use figurative language. You'll see their books are peppered with simile, metaphor, puns, and idioms. Imagine the first time a child reads *Amelia Bedelia*, with her talk of dressing the turkey or drawing the shades! You'll let your children know that sometimes when they're reading along, they'll find themselves thinking, "What? Huh?" and in those instances, they will probably want to reread and to think, "Might the author have been doing something creative-crazy?" You'll want to let your children know that when authors write with especially playful language, they're hoping the reader will notice what they've done and pay special attention to the language and the meaning. It's kind of like the author is pulling on a reader's sleeve, saying, "Notice this!" When authors do that, readers are supposed to stop and think, "Wait a minute! That's not what it *really* means!" Then they use what's happening in the story to think about what would make sense.

Bend II begins with you announcing a new "Research Bulletin about Second-Grade Readers," alerting children to this new, important reading research you just found. You'll ham this up a bit, excitedly pulling out the bulletin, printed on a piece of paper, and you'll read aloud:

Researchers have found that the books second-graders read often contain language that is used in playful and inventive ways. Second-graders who are especially skilled readers pay attention when a writer has used words in special ways because they know that those passages require extra thought.

You might ask children, "So what do we do with this news?" as you rally them around the new work of the bend. In this second bend, you'll bring second-graders in on the fact that their books will be more and more full of playful inventive language, and part of being a skilled second-grade reader is that it is important to notice when an author has done something special and to work hard to really understand what the author is trying to say. You can show students examples from the books they know, such as *Owl Moon* by Jane Yolen, which your children may have studied if you teach Units of Study in Opinion, Information, and Narrative Writing. "Listen," you'll say to your children, and you might read aloud passages such as this one:

The moon made his face
into a silver mask.
Then he called:
"Whoo-whoo-who-who-who-whooooooo,"
the sound of a Great Horned Owl.

If your teaching goes well, then your children will begin making their own reading-writing connections. As this bend in the unit unfolds, you'll call children's attention, above all, to the ways in which the authors of the books they are reading use comparison as a way to convey meaning. You'll let your second-graders know that when an author really wants readers to be able to imagine something, the author will sometimes describe the object by comparing it to something that is actually very different. Using literary language, a safety pin can be compared to a fish. The author expects readers to bring the safety pin and the fish together into a brand new, made-for-the-moment meaning. Of course, if you have been teaching poetry in your writing workshop, your

AN ORIENTATION TO THE UNIT

children will be pros at this work. And certainly you'll reinforce your children's study of comparisons by reading aloud. You might start by using Molly Bang's classic, *When Sophie Gets Angry*, reading, "Sophie is a volcano, ready to explode" and discussing what the author really means by this.

At the end of this bend, you'll want to connect this reading work to writing. The session begins by having students recall familiar writing strategies and then guiding them to search their texts for instances when other authors have used these strategies. You'll teach children that when readers notice what the author is doing, they can try to name it and think, "What special meaning does the author want me to get?" You'll end this bend by allowing children to use what they've noticed and learned as readers in their own writing—inviting them to really write. You may say, "For partner time today, you'll do something a bit different—you will write! Together with your partner, take out your writing folders and try to see if you can add some literary language to your writing. You can borrow some of the phrases you have found in your books and jotted down on your Post-its, or you can make up your own. Sometimes the very best writers borrow a phrase or two from other books." You might coach students as they use their notes to practice adding literary language to their own writing.

Bend III: Meeting the Challenges of Longer Books

Often students are reading with their eyes but nothing registers in their brains. You may alert children by saying, "I am serious about this. Those researchers who study second-grade readers have pointed out what a problem it is when a reader is reading along, thinking things are hunky dory, when really there is an emergency. The story is not getting through to the reader's brain! If the reader doesn't know there's a problem, he might go right through the book, finish it, and say he's done without even realizing he hasn't *read* it at all. He just looked at it!" You will then teach students strategies to use when this happens, such as using Post-its to keep themselves accountable for understanding what is happening and slowing down to reread.

Bend III launches like Bend II, with a breaking news bulletin. Again, you will get readers excited for the work of the third bend. You'll read aloud the bulletin to the class, introducing a new challenge that comes with longer books in second grade:

Researchers report that, because the books second-graders read are much longer than those read by younger readers, second-grade readers face a

new risk. As second-grade readers read, there is a clear risk that they can lose the storyline.

In the third bend you'll also launch same-book partnerships. Up until now, partners may have been reading the same book, but many were likely reading different books based on their levels. It is probably the case that all students are ready to read the same book as their partners. The same-book partnerships will also help launch the new work of this bend, as partners will serve as a resource for helping each other keep track of what is happening in longer texts. You might tell children, "Often, with longer books, it's easy to lose the story, and sometimes students don't even realize it's happening! It helps to have strategies and a partner to keep track of the w-h-o-l-e story." Students will be introduced to Post-its to track their reading, which you'll teach them to use like a trail of breadcrumbs. You'll help students learn to use Post-its to remember all the important events in their longer books.

Bend IV: Tackling Goals in the Company of Others

This last bend is really what makes this unit special. It is a time when the tables are turned and students take on the role of a researcher. The bend starts with students doing some self-assessment and setting a goal for their reading work. Throughout the bend, children will coach and support one another in reaching their goals.

You'll set students up to work in clubs with others who share similar goals. The clubs might be categorized as the Fluency Club, the Literary Language Club, and the Keeping Track of Longer Books Club, to address the work of the past three bends. You'll want to help students be thoughtful and honest when choosing their goals.

Logistically, students will be meeting with their clubs four to five times, every day of this bend. This will replace partner time, just for this bend. During this time, they will be in groups of three to four students. Each of the three big goals might have a few clubs. For example, you might have two fluency clubs of four students each if eight students have chosen fluency as their goal.

Once students are in these clubs, you'll have an opportunity to teach them ways to work together, including how to organize themselves and create routines. You'll teach your students the importance of sharing honestly what they are doing well and what they'd like to get better at, and of making communal plans to reach their goals. They'll gather resources and ideas, make plans, use tools, and practice strategies as they collaborate to achieve their goals.

When students are working together in clubs, it's a great time to teach them how to give each other helpful feedback on progress toward their goals. They can use the anchor charts to guide each other in their work.

The unit ends with a celebration in which you'll position students to play the role of a researcher. They'll have a chance to release their own news bulletins to teach others about reading. You might invite your readers to join you on the rug, sitting with their goal clubs. You might say to children, "You have done such powerful research that it's worth publishing. I'm thinking that we can share our research with other readers! Perhaps we can put the news bulletins you created in the school paper, or send them home as a memo, so all readers can know about your reading research and use it to become better readers." Then, you can have each club read their research news bulletin to the rest of the class. When your celebration is complete, collect the research students have done and publish it!

ASSESSMENT

Assess students' reading levels with running records.

Begin the unit by analyzing your most recent running records. In January, students reading on benchmark will be reading levels K and L. At any point, you may conduct running records (either formal or informal) to determine whether students have moved up in reading levels and to assess whether their rereading, word solving, and fluency have improved. Always be on the lookout for signals that students are ready to move up levels, so you can pull these students aside to assess. Your assessments will help you identify specific goals that you can address in your conferences, small-group, and whole-class lessons.

Mining running records to analyze the miscues of readers below benchmark will be especially important. Many of your readers often need additional support integrating sources of information as they approach unfamiliar words. Running records allow you to see what strategies a child is using to word solve and what the reader needs support with. Is the reader using meaning, structure, and visual information to solve words? Is the reader using multiple sources of information to solve words with more efficiency? Does the reader need additional support solving multisyllabic words with a variety of inflectional endings, prefixes, and suffixes? Is the reader able to self-correct at the point of error when the error disrupts meaning?

Consider additional assessments for students below benchmark.

By now, most, if not all, of your students have probably mastered 200 high-frequency words. For some students this still may be an area of need. Continue to use an assessment, such as the TCRWP High-Frequency Words Assessment, to see what words to target in small group lessons with these students. Make sure that they are practicing these words daily, during word study as well as reading and writing workshop.

It's also important to ensure that your students' phonics knowledge is increasing. We suggest you continue to conduct a spelling inventory, such as the inventory in *Words Their Way*, to identify areas of phonics and word study to target in your instruction. For example, if you have students reading below grade level, especially students below levels I and J, it will be important to conduct a spelling inventory in order to assess what spelling features they have under control. It may be that these students struggle with short and long vowel sounds. You'll want to pull these students in a small group to work on these skills. You can refer to Chapter 6 in *A Guide to the Reading Workshop, Primary Grades* for more information on where to find and how to administer these assessments.

Use formative assessments to plan instruction throughout the unit of study.

Throughout the unit, you'll also conduct other types of formative assessments that inform your instruction. As you pull together shared reading fluency groups or strategy groups to work on decoding and figuring out the meaning of new words, keep track of the growth your students are making. Your small group and conference notes are important assessment tools to guide your instruction. When looking over your conference notes, you may notice that many students have a similar need, and you can gather those students into a small group to teach together. As you take small group notes and look back over them, you may notice the progress some students have made, and you may also notice students who seem stuck and need additional support.

Post-its are another powerful assessment tool. Students will be using Post-its to mark passages throughout their books. Look over these Post-its to see if students are marking important parts and understanding what is happening in the story. You may use students' Post-its to plan small group work and individual conferences to support comprehension.

In addition to these tools, reading logs offer a window into students' reading volume and stamina. Noting and analyzing reading volume can inform your teaching. Students who are reading level J books should be reading about thirty books a week, as a level J book takes about fifteen minutes to read. Students reading level L books may read about eight books a week, as it takes closer to twenty to twenty-five minutes to read a book at that level. Level M readers may be reading closer to six books in a week, as these books take thirty or more minutes to read. Especially during Bend I, where fluency is a big focus, spending time looking at students' reading logs can provide valuable information about reading pace and volume.

Tailor your curriculum according to the data you collect.

Your running records, conferring notes, student Post-its, logs, and other sources of information will help you make decisions about your plans for this unit of study and others. If you find that a group of your second-graders are reading below the benchmark during this unit, then you may want to refer to *If . . . Then . . . Curriculum: Assessment-Based Instruction, Grades K–2* as a resource. The unit titled "Word Detectives Use All They Know to Solve Words" is a foundational skills unit geared for readers reading levels E/F/G and can serve as an extension to this unit. You might decide to use this unit as a supplement to guide small-group work and function as extra support for students who need it, or you might decide to select particular lessons or bends and add them to your unit plan.

GETTING READY

Gather books, poems, charts, songs, and more for your students to read.

For this unit of study, your students will be transitioning from reading nonfiction books into reading fiction and poetry. You will then want your library to highlight and support students in quickly and effectively finding just-right books and texts that they are interested in.

At the beginning of the unit, you may decide to place on each table baskets filled with poems, songs, and other texts that are chock-full of literary language. Reading poems and songs will give students opportunities to practice reading and rereading a variety of texts and to work on their fluency. Additionally, these baskets of poetry can help readers at all levels practice noticing and understanding literary language. From these baskets, you may select poems by some favorite poets, such as the poem "Aquarium" by Valerie Worth, "Lullaby" by Kristine O'Connell George, and "Way Down in the Music" by Eloise Greenfield. You also may choose some anthologies of children's poetry, such as *It's Raining Pigs and Noodles* by Jack Prelutsky or *Climb Inside a Poem* by Georgia Heard and Lester Laminack. You may also find more through online sources such as the children's section of the Poetry Foundation's website.

You may also include in these baskets with some shorter picture books as well, such as *When Sophie Gets Angry—Really, Really Angry . . .* by Molly Bang, *Lilly's Purple Plastic Purse* by Kevin Henkes, *Owl Moon* by Jane Yolen, *Ruthie and the Not So Teeny Tiny Lie* by Laura Rankin, and *Houndsley and Catina* by James Howe. These picture books are full of metaphors, similes, word play, and other types of literary language that would be wonderful for your students to read, study, and discuss, especially for those not quite ready to launch into longer chapter books.

Toward the end of this unit of study, students will be shopping for the same book as their partner. We suggest you plan ahead for this, perhaps by gathering duplicate books to fill a section of the library. You may choose to rubber band these duplicate books together and display them as sets. That way, when students book shop, they can easily find these books and share them with their partners.

Select and gather books and texts for minilessons and guided reading.

As you collect texts for this unit, you will want to find books that will help reinforce the skills of the unit, as well as work on skills that your readers need to meet their reading levels. To support the fluency work in the unit, we use *Houndsley and Catina* by James Howe, but you can also use many other books. You will want to choose one that is slightly above most of your students' independent reading levels and one that you can use to teach other skills, such as understanding literary language and keeping track of longer books. Many chapter books at levels L and M will work well.

In order to support students with the work of literary language, we use *Happy Like Soccer* by Maribeth Boelts, but other books such as *When Sophie Gets Angry—Really, Really Angry . . .* by Molly Bang, *Lilly's Purple Plastic Purse* by Kevin Henkes, *Owl Moon* by Jane Yolen, *Ruthie and the Not So Teeny Tiny Lie* by Laura Rankin, and *Come on Rain* by Karen Hesse are also lovely choices.

It is a major hurdle for many second-graders to keep track of longer books, to follow a long storyline across many chapters. Choosing books to help support this skill is a bit tricky. Series books like Frog and Toad by Arnold Lobel and Poppleton by Cynthia Rylant may seem like they would work well because they are longer. However, in these texts each chapter is a stand-alone story, so students won't have opportunities to practice carrying a storyline across an entire text. We use *Minnie and Moo Go Dancing* by Denys Cazet, but many chapter books with one long story would work as well. Some of our favorites are *Iris and Walter* by Elissa Haden Guest, *Mercy Watson* by Kate DiCamillo, and *Pinky and Rex* by James Howe.

For students below benchmark, guided reading will be one type of small group you will be doing to help move them along. You will want to think about the reading levels of your students and select sets of guided reading texts that will be a level above their independent reading levels. You will want to prepare a few sets at each level to support the guided reading work across the unit.

Another source for guided reading material might be a few pages from a junior novel or nonfiction book that matches the level of the students. If your assessment information shows a group of students are having difficulty with a particular comprehension skill, recall a good part of a longer story where this can be taught. While this passage might only be 100–200 words, it will home in on a comprehension skill you want your readers to practice and master.

Create and prepare to distribute special tools.

Throughout the unit, as in the past units, you will want to support students in using tools they have already made and created. For example, you will want to reinforce the use of student reading logs to support volume. You will also want to continue to make the charts available to students. Be sure they can still reference charts from Units 1 and 2 and the new charts you create across this unit.

There will be some new tools you could create and distribute as well. In Bend II, students will be keeping track of the literary language they find in texts. Some teachers give students a plastic baggie, and as they find examples of literary language, they collect them on Post-its and add them to their baggies. Some teachers give students a special piece of paper and ask students to collect literary language on their special pieces of paper, which they store in their book baggies. Either way, it will be important to create a space for children to collect literary language phrases, so they can analyze them with their partners.

In the final bend, students will be working with clubs and each club will need various tools. Students will need a club planning sheet, Post-its, and copies of the charts and tools they will be creating themselves to help run their clubs.

Use the read-aloud plan in the back of this book to help you prepare for one read-aloud across a couple of days as well as others, across the unit.

In the back of this book, after the last session, you will find a plan for reading aloud *Minnie and Moo Go Dancing* by Denys Cadet. Of course, you'll read many other books as well during this unit, and we recommend you choose books that are inviting and engaging and will help you demonstrate key skills in this unit. That way, when students go off during independent reading to work on their own books, they'll have a model to support them. *Minnie and Moo Go Dancing* is the kind of book that does the trick.

Minnie and Moo are best friends and cows that live on a farm. The farmer is having a party at his house, and Minnie and Moo get upset they aren't invited. They decide to dress up like humans and go to the party. Their plan works until hamburgers are served at the party, and Minnie and Moo think they may be next on the menu, so they run off. It is a book that will make students laugh and give them lots of opportunities to practice many comprehension skills. As you read the book aloud, you'll engage children in skill work such as previewing, predicting, and growing ideas about the characters and story. The skills you will teach will echo the teaching you will do inside the unit of study. You will notice that this read-aloud plan and the corresponding prompts will allow you to give your students a wonderful read-aloud experience, and you will be able to use these transferable prompts to plan subsequent read-aloud lessons across the remainder of the unit.

Select books that have engaging, complex stories that will be fun to talk and think about.

We chose *Minnie and Moo* as this unit's read-aloud text for several reasons. For starters, it is very funny and engaging for students. While often read-alouds are above the end-of-year grade level benchmark, this text is a level L, which is *at* benchmark level. While much of the time your read-alouds will be with above grade level texts, it is also important to read aloud texts at students' independent reading level for a few reasons. One reason is to model the thinking skills you want students doing during independent reading time, in a text similar to the ones that they will be reading. Another reason is to show the value of a variety of texts, at a variety of levels. You want students to know and value *all* types of texts.

Another reason we chose this book is that it has one long storyline. This means that your students will need to do a bit of work to accumulate details across a longer text. This is something that they will be working on independently. During the read-aloud, you will demonstrate and help kids practice tracking the story. This will support students as they continue to tackle complex texts on their own. In addition to that, this book is full of literary language, with metaphors, similes, and plays on words. Discussing the literary language from this book will also support your students in doing so with their own books.

Use the five-day plan in the back of this book to help you prepare for shared reading.

In this unit, we outline a shared reading five-day plan using *Happy Like Soccer* by Maribeth Boelts. It is a level M text, which is slightly above the K/L benchmark for this time of year. You can find this plan after the read-aloud section in this book. Like the other five-day plans from previous units, this plan will help move you through key foundational skills that your students will need mid-year in second grade.

Happy Like Soccer is a great choice to start with in shared reading for this unit. It is a story about Sierra, who wants her aunt to be able to come to her soccer games to watch her play. However, her aunt works on Saturdays and the games are never near where she lives. One day her aunt gets a day off and is able to come watch her play, but the game gets canceled because of rain. Sierra and her soccer coach come up with a creative way to solve her problem.

You'll notice that the shared reading plan we offer coaches children to preview the text and predict what might happen, as well as to draw on some more advanced word-solving skills, such as using prefixes and suffixes and breaking apart multisyllabic words. This book is also filled with literary language that you will help students understand and use. Students will also work to gain deep understanding of the text. Each day, you'll engage the class in a discussion or an activity to extend the text. For example, you'll ask the class to help you retell the important parts in sequence using literary language, or to help you write a book review. After you finish *Happy Like Soccer*, you'll select other texts to use in shared reading. You can follow the five-day plan and transfer and practice these same types of skills in other texts as you engage kids in shared reading throughout the unit.

ONLINE DIGITAL RESOURCES

A variety of resources to accompany this and the other Grade 2 Units of Study for Teaching Reading are available in the Online Resources, including charts and examples of student work shown throughout *Bigger Books Mean Amping Up Reading Power*, as well as links to other electronic resources. Offering daily support for your teaching, these materials will help you provide a structured learning environment that fosters independence and self-direction.

To access and download all the digital resources for the Grade 2 Units of Study for Teaching Reading:

1. Go to **www.heinemann.com** and click the link in the upper right to log in. (If you do not have an account yet, you will need to create one.)
2. **Enter the following registration code** in the box to register your product: RUOS_Gr2
3. Under **My Online Resources**, click the link for the **Grade 2 Reading Units of Study**.
4. The digital resources are available under the headings; click a file name to download.

(You may keep copies of these resources on up to six of your own computers or devices. By downloading the files you acknowledge that they are for your individual or classroom use and that neither the resources nor the product code will be distributed or shared.)

Reading with Fluency BEND I

Session 1

Rehearsing Reading Voices

IN THIS SESSION, you'll teach children that reading aloud can help their in-their-head reading voices.

GETTING READY

- Give students new book baggies with fiction books at their independent reading levels. They'll need to have chosen those books before today's workshop.
- Create a new anchor chart for the bend titled "Making Your Reading More Fluent." Prepare to add the first strategy Post-it note—"Reread aloud and in your head" (see Teaching and Active Engagement).
- Display an enlarged copy of the first page of *Owl Moon* by Jane Yolen with a document camera (see Teaching and Active Engagement).
- Place Post-it notes at students' reading spots to mark parts of their books (see Link).
- Place new reading logs in folders at students' reading spots (see Link).
- Write the lyrics to "Read Parts of Our Books," to be sung to the tune of "The Wheels on the Bus," on chart paper (see Share).

MINILESSON

CONNECTION

Explain that reading researchers know second grade is an important time for reading development, especially for the shift from oral to silent reading.

"Readers, you know how there are scientists who study bees, and there are scientists who study hurricanes. Well, there are also scientists who study *reading*. There are professors of reading, and to study reading they go into classrooms just like ours, with their clipboards and their pens behind their ears, and they watch and listen to kids reading.

"*And* there are whole books about second-grade readers, because reading scientists have decided that second grade is pretty much the most important grade for reading growth. As we start this new unit of study, you need to know that one of the most important things those scientists have found is that second grade is the year when lots of kids start to read silently."

Emphasize that readers rely on an internalized voice.

"Reading researchers have found that second-grade readers have a reading voice in their heads. Sometimes it is the voice of the story, or the voice of the teaching book, or the voice of the poem. Sometimes it is a joyful voice, or a surprised voice, or an angry voice. But it is no longer the voice of the beginning reader who/is/trying/to/get/the/words/right. Instead, it is the voice of smooth, fluent reading.

"Reading with fluency (that's what the researchers call it) is one of the *most important skills* for second-grade readers, because reading fluently helps you understand what you're reading."

Name the teaching point.

"Today I want to teach you a magical thing that reading scientists have found. They have discovered that *rereading*—especially rereading out loud—is the best way to change the voice inside a reader's head. And that voice is everything."

TEACHING AND ACTIVE ENGAGEMENT

Suggest that by learning to read aloud well, students can lift the level of their internal reading voices.

"Did you know that there are high school kids who read one piece of writing—the *same* piece of writing—every single day for the first month of school? The reason teachers have them do this is because teachers know that being able to read one thing *really* well can change the reading voice in your head. It's the power of *rereading*, over and over. Let's try it right now."

I unveiled the new fluency anchor chart and added the new strategy.

We recommend against calculating a child's words per minute before children read at level J. Second grade is the first time words per minute should be assessed. During this year, through a focus on meaning, intonation, and phrasing, students generally increase from 55–85 words per minute early in the year to 75–105 words per minute later in the year.

ANCHOR CHART

Making Your Reading More Fluent

- **Reread aloud and in your head.**

Channel kids to listen to themselves read a passage from a familiar text aloud into pretend conch shells.

"Readers, have you ever spoken into one of those big conch shells that you see at the beach? When you speak into those shells, you can hear your voice as if it's in an echo chamber. With your hands, can you make a conch shell in front of your mouth?" I made one, using my left hand to make the inner tube of the shell, which I set against the cup of my right hand.

FIG. 1–1 Finn uses a pretend conch shell to practice his reading voice.

"I am going to really listen to my voice as I read this story. Do the same—hold up your shell to your mouth and listen to your own voice as you read. Let's read with our best reading voices." I displayed the beginning of *Owl Moon* by Jane Yolen.

> It was late one winter night,
>
> long past my bedtime,
>
> when Pa and I went owling.
>
> There was no wind.
>
> The trees stood still
>
> as giant statues.
>
> And the moon was so bright
>
> the sky seemed to shine.
>
> Somewhere behind us
>
> a train whistle blew,
>
> long and low,
>
> like a sad, sad song.

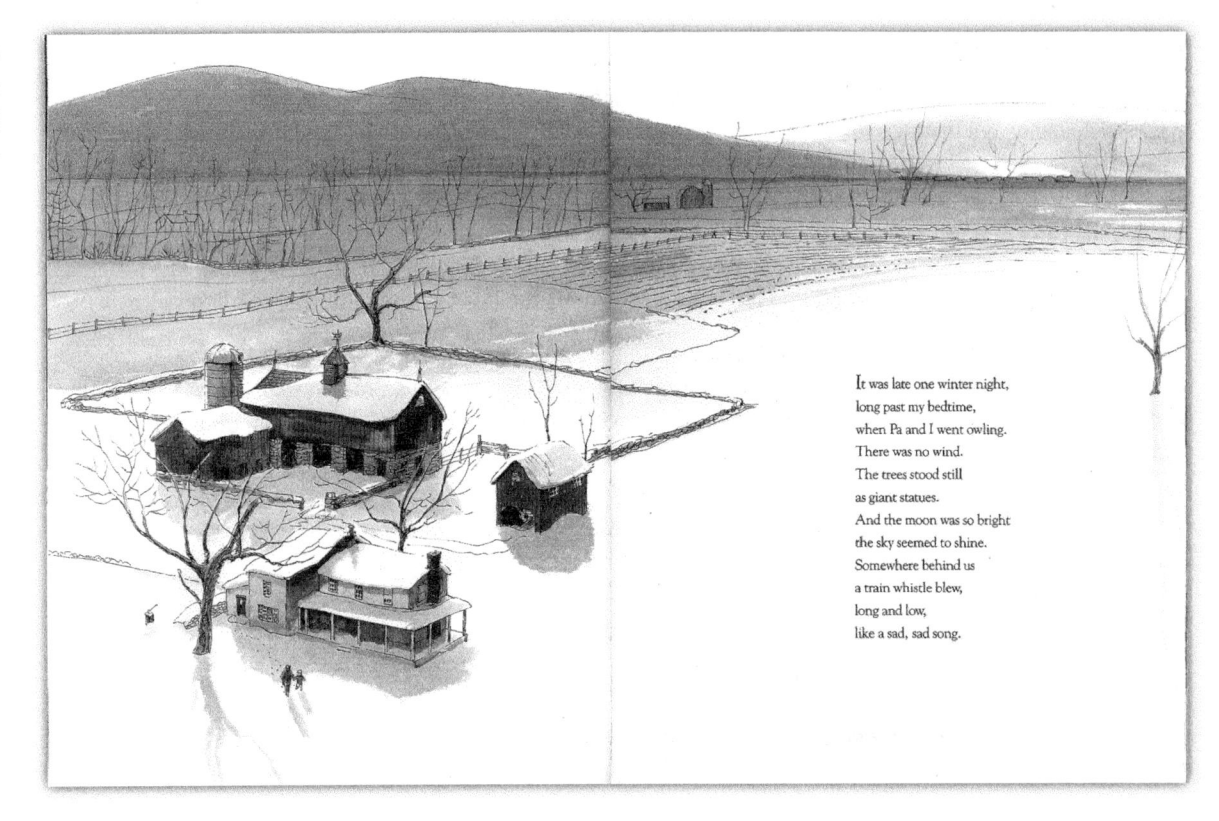

Demonstrate rereading, emphasizing how readers envision the story and match their voices to what is happening as they read aloud.

After most of the children had finished reading the page together, I said, "Now let's reread, this time making our reading voices even better. Let me give you a tip." I leaned in, leaving a pause to give my words more weight. "You need to *see* what's happening, *to experience* what's happening in your mind, when you read the words. This time, really make your voice match what's happening." I held a pretend conch shell to my mouth and encouraged the class to join in as I reread *Owl Moon*, this time reading with heightened feeling.

"Did you picture the snowy winter night? Can you see those tall, still trees?" The children nodded. "And the moon? Is it *so* bright you're almost squinting?" Several kids squinted their eyes, picturing the scene.

"I noticed that your voices sounded so expressive and smooth when you read that time. Just imagine if we practiced it a few more times out loud!"

Choose a familiar text to reread. We harken back to a mentor text students studied during an earlier writing unit, but you may choose any story children love.

Invite children to reread the passage once more, this time silently, matching their inner voices to the reading they did aloud.

"Now, go back and make that in-your-head, silent reading voice sound just as it did when you read aloud just now. Even though you'll be reading silently, really listen. Make your voice help you actually *see* what's happening in your mind." I dropped my voice to a whisper, "Ready? Go."

LINK

Recruit help thinking about how this repeated practice can transfer to independent reading. Encourage kids to select passages from their own books to reread aloud.

"Readers, in a minute you'll get to head off to your reading spots. You'll be reading silently, like you usually do during reading time, but as you read, make sure that you can hear that in-your-head reading voice. Use Post-its to mark parts of the text that you think will be especially perfect for reading out loud, because later I'm going to ask you to reread those parts to yourself and your partner. Remember, rereading a bit out loud helps to make your silent reading voice stronger.

"Meanwhile, second-graders, I want to tell you that all the second-grade teachers at this school got together and decided that you are old enough to begin keeping logs that show how much reading you have done. When you get back to your reading spot, you'll see that I have given each of you a folder holding your new reading log. When you start a book today, write down the title of the book and today's date. You can decide if you want to keep track of page numbers or just when you begin and finish books.

"These logs will give us a way to study how much reading you're doing in school and at home. We're doing this because nothing will help you become a stronger reader more than reading, reading, reading! So get started!"

Name: Hannah				
Date	School/Home	Title	Minutes	Parent's initials
1-5-15	S	Poppleton	38	
1-5-15	H	Iris and Walter—the sleepover	30	*init*
1-6-15	S	Iris and Walter—and Baby Rose	41	
1-6-15	H	Mercy Watson to the Rescue	25	QV
1-7-15	S	Mercy Watson to the Rescue	37	
1-7-15	H	Annie and Snowball and the Wintry Freeze	36	QV
1-8-15	S	Mr. Putter and Tabby Feed the Fish	37	
1-8-15	H	Houndsley and Catina and the Quiet time	32	QV
1-9-15	S	Nate the Great	44	
1-9-15	H	Nate the Great	30	QV

FIG. 1–2 You can use reading logs, to learn more about students reading pace and fluency.

The decision to ask kids to keep reading logs is one that you and your colleagues will need to make. We generally don't ask second-graders at the start of the year to do this because it sometimes seems to us that when they are reading shorter books, they end up spending more time recording the title and author of a book than reading it! Therefore, for a time, children simply make a check mark when they complete one more book, and a new check mark each time they reread the book. By this time of year, however, many of your students are reading books that require more than one day to complete, and they are less apt to reread, cover to cover. This is why we suggest launching a system of logging reading that we use throughout the upper grades. It's only worth launching reading logs, however, if you can commit to helping students keep them and study them.

SESSION 1: REHEARSING READING VOICES

CONFERRING AND SMALL-GROUP WORK

Moving Quickly from Reader to Reader

Recruit energy for the new work of the unit.

At the start of any unit, it's a good idea to travel quickly among the kids, recruiting their active enthusiastic engagement in the unit. That won't be hard for you to do today, because you'll be asking kids to do work they love: reading books and poems they've chosen, and anticipating sharing those texts with friends.

As you circulate among students, you may want to seed children's reading baggies with some books that are especially perfect for reading aloud. You might surprise children by sneaking books you know they'll love into their baggies, or go from child to child with very quick book introductions to talk up new books. For example, you might begin reading *The Ghost Eye Tree* by Bill Martin, savoring the way the tone of the book escalates, becoming more intense as the story continues, almost like a drumroll, and then stop part way through and say, "I just know you'll love this book, would you like to read it?"

In addition, you'll probably have moved some youngsters up a notch in text complexity, and may, therefore, want to provide book introductions to start them off well. If you have a few kids reading the first book in the same series, you may want to gather those kids, tell them a bit about the series, and perhaps read a few pages aloud. Even something as quick as that can set readers up for success with a new series.

Confer with students briefly to provide feedback and light coaching.

It's also important to let readers know that you are interested in that silent voice in their heads. Of course, you can't hear that voice, so you'll need to settle for hearing them read books aloud. You might say, "Readers, when I tap you on your shoulder, read the part you are on aloud for me so I can hear the way you are making the book come to life with your voice."

You may want to try some quick two- to three-minute, "dip in/dip out" conferences, during which you quickly name one thing a child is doing well and one new strategy for the student to try. For example, after listening to one child read, you might say, "You're reading at a nice pace: not too fast, and not too slow. That's great work. Can you try to reread with some more expression? Keep going and try that now." Or you may say, "I saw how you started your book, scooping up words. Don't forget to keep that going." These conferences are meant to be quick.

You might turn some of these individual conferences into table conferences. You could say to the entire table, "Can I have your attention? Carla was just working on her out-loud reading voice. Remember, reading out loud will help your in-your-head reading voice. All of you, try doing what Carla is working on. I'll come around and help you as you get started." These table conferences should give kids a teaching point and possibly an example. Ultimately, the goal is to get the group to practice right there on the spot with some light coaching from you. These quick table conferences allow you to see more students for shorter intervals.

MID-WORKSHOP TEACHING
Rereading a Passage the Way It Wants to Be Read

"Readers, can I stop you for a second?" I waited for children to look up. "Now is the time to choose a part of your book that is especially perfect for reading aloud. Pick one now if you haven't already and point to it."

After children had located passages, I said, "Later, you'll reread this part to a partner, but for now, take a little time to practice it. Reread it to yourself, trying to picture what it is saying, the same way you did when we read *Owl Moon*. Try reading it different ways to figure out how that passage really *wants* to be read. Right now, reread that passage aloud to yourself into your conch shell.

"Now the challenge is to continue reading on silently in your book with that voice in your head, reading and rereading the rest of the book, and all your books, like that."

SHARE

Making Readers' Voices Sing

Sing a class song together, connecting it to the rereading work readers (and singers) do to make their voices sound smooth.

I gathered students back in the meeting area, each sitting beside his or her partner, books in hand. "Those research scientists uncovered some pretty important information about reading, do you remember it? They said *rereading*—practicing a bit out loud—is the best way to make your in your head voices stronger.

"Well, here's something that may sound surprising. You're not the only ones who reread to make your voice stronger, smoother, and sound just right. Singers do, too. That's right! Singers are readers. They read and reread to make their voices sound exactly right. They practice out loud, they hum in their head, they sing to themselves, and they sing to other people. Right now, let's work together to make our voices really *sing*!"

I revealed the lyrics I had written on chart paper. "I'm sure most of you know the tune of this song. It sounds just like 'The Wheels on the Bus.' If you know it, join me!" I started the verse as children chimed in:

(To the tune of "The Wheels on the Bus"):

Read parts of our books again and again
out loud and in our heads
out loud and in our heads
Read parts of our books again and again
to make our reading smoooooth!

FIG. 1–3 The "Rereading Song" is available on the online resources.

"Don't forget—the best way to make silent voices smoother is to reread. Let's practice once more aloud. This time, you take the lead!" I nudged, as the class sang the verse again. "I bet this song will be in your head for the rest of the day! As you sing it silently to yourself, make your in-your-head reading voice just as *smoooooth*!"

Transition students into partnerships, rallying them to reread together in smooth voices.

"I wonder if you can use those same smooth voices to read together with your partners. Right now, choose a few parts to reread together. Then practice reading out loud a bit, making your voices *almost* sing!" I moved from partnership to partnership, listening in as students read together.

Session 2

Scooping Up Words into Phrases

IN THIS SESSION, you'll teach children that readers scoop up words into phrases and notice punctuation so that their reading makes sense and sounds right.

GETTING READY

- Enlarge a copy of a song for students to sing. We use the "Rereading Song" (see Connection).
- Display page 1 of *Houndsley and Catina* to the class, perhaps using a document camera (see Teaching).
- Direct each partnership to page 2 from *Houndsley and Catina* as they come to the rug (see Active Engagement).
- Display the anchor chart "Making Your Reading More Fluent" and prepare to add the strategy Post-it—"Scoop words into longer phrases" (see Link).
- Create an anchor chart titled "Partners Reread Together to . . . ," so that it is ready to refer to, and prepare to add the strategy—"Practice out loud and try to picture what's happening" (see Share).

One of the ways you'll remove scaffolding over time is by going from clearly pointing under the words as children read them, to pointing in an approximate way, to just touching the first word of the new line of print.

MINILESSON

CONNECTION

Rally students to read with more fluent voices by chorally singing the song from the previous share.

"Yesterday, you worked on being the kind of readers who reread, a bit out loud and then in your head, to make your reading voices smooth—almost like singing. Let's sing our rereading song once more today!" I clipped the lyrics to the easel and motioned for the class to sing aloud again to the tune of "The Wheels on the Bus."

> *Read parts of our books again and again,*
>
> *out loud and in our heads,*
>
> *out loud and in our heads.*
>
> *Read parts of our book again and again,*
>
> *to make our reading* smoooooth!

Recruit children to read the words of the song in longer phrases.

"Beautiful! What smooth, fluent voices! I bet that you can use those same voices to *read* the words of the song, as you would read the words of a story or a poem or an information book. So this time, let's read each line, saying the words in nice, big scoops." I took my pointer and swept under each line, coaching students to read in longer phrases.

❖ **Name the teaching point.**

"Today I want to teach you that you can make your reading voice just as smooth as your singing voice by reading in longer phrases. You can scoop up more words at a time by noticing the punctuation. Then, you can check that your reading sounds right."

TEACHING

Demonstrate reading using punctuation cues to scoop the text into longer, meaningful phrases, pausing explicitly to help students see and hear how you've parsed the text. Then, stop and check that your reading makes sense and sounds right.

"Let's make our reading voices sound just as smooth as the voices we use to sing!" I displayed the first page of *Houndsley and Catina* with the document camera. "Watch how I scoop up more words at a time, noticing when the punctuation signals me to take a breath. That way, I can read in phrases that make sense and sound right."

"Let me think about how this should sound." I read the first sentence aloud, in choppy, two-word phrases.

Catina wanted/to be/a writer.

"Hmm, . . . That sounded pretty choppy and not at all like the smooth singing voice I used to read earlier. How can I read that to make it sound right? I know punctuation helps! Oh yes, I see a period at the end, right here. That's a clue," I said as I pointed to the period at the end of the first sentence. "Okay, let me read it again, this time reading the whole sentence in one big scoop, one breath." I took a deep breath, then reread the sentence in one swoop.

Catina wanted to be a writer.

I turned to the class, "Smoother?" They nodded. "Does it sound right?" Again, they nodded. "And it makes sense, too!" Then, I took my marker and drew a curved line underneath the first sentence to signify one whole phrase.

Teach readers the importance of considering meaning and syntax to phrase longer sentences, especially when there is no punctuation to cue pauses.

"Let me keep going. Yikes! The next sentence looks like a long one. I'll need to make sure I look out for punctuation marks and check that I read it in a way that makes sense and sounds right." I slid my finger underneath the sentence, stopping at the first punctuation mark.

SESSION 2: SCOOPING UP WORDS INTO PHRASES

"I see a comma here. That tells me to scoop all the words before the comma together. At the comma, I'll take a breath," I said, as I pointed to the first phrase leading up to the comma:

Every evening after dinner,

I read the first part of the sentence in one scoop, cueing the phrase with my marker.

"The next part is a long one! And there's no punctuation until the end of the page! Let me try reading it in one big scoop." I read the next part of the sentence, all in one breath:

. . . she would make herself a cup of ginger tea and sit down to write another chapter in her book.

I let out an exhale, as if winded. "Did that sound right?" Students shook their heads, no. "I ran out of breath, didn't I? This is a challenging one. Okay, let me try it again. I'll need to listen and think about what words make sense together and sound right. If you have an idea, put a thumb up when I should pause and take a breath." I began to reread:

. . . she would make herself a cup of ginger tea . . .

The students started to signal that I should pause. "Do these words make sense and sound right together?" The children agreed they did. I marked the text, scooping the words. "Okay, let me reread and then try to scoop up the rest of the sentence." I reread from the start of the line, taking a breath to separate each phrase:

Every evening after dinner,

she would make herself a cup of ginger tea

and sit down to write another chapter in her book.

The students raised their thumbs in unison as I reached the end of the line. "Yep. That period at the end definitely signals me to stop here." I marked the final phrase.

Debrief in a way that is transferable to another text and another day.

"Readers, did you see what I just did? Did you see how I used the punctuation to signal when to take a breath and how to scoop up the words? Then, when a part was extra long and didn't have punctuation, I thought about which words would make sense and sound right when scooped up together."

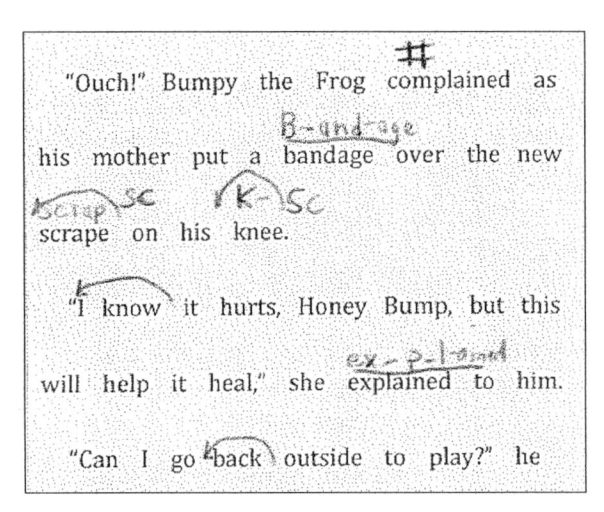

FIG. 2–1 Note the pausing and rereading in this running record. If students' running records look like this, this bend will be especially important.

Make this reading of the text seem like it's too much for one breath. Ask the kids if it sounds right, and expect a protest, leading you to reread, adding a pause and a breath.

You may choose to give children a photocopy of the read-aloud page so they can write directly on it, using a highlighter or marker to divide longer sentences into phrases. This creates a phrase-cued text, in which boundaries are explicitly marked to help students move from word-by-word reading to reading in meaningful phrases. The aim here is not to teach kids that readers regularly mark their own books, of course, but instead to provide visual support for them as they get a feel for how to do this.

ACTIVE ENGAGEMENT

Remind students to use punctuation and rereading to help decide the phrasing of the text. Coach partnerships as they do this work together.

I quickly directed students to page 2 of *Houndsley and Catina*. "Now it's your turn to try! Place page 2 of *Houndsley and Catina* between you and your partner. I want you to read this page. You might read it silently to yourself first, and then read a bit out loud together. Then, work with your partner to decide how you'll scoop up the words so you don't read one/or/two words/at a/time, but in longer phrases, so it sounds like you're telling a story. Use your finger to draw the scoops underneath each phrase. Remember punctuation can help. Ready, *go*!"

As students worked, I walked around and coached, looking for an example to share with the class. "Readers, let's reread this page together and see if we scooped phrases like Joel and Carly." Students turned their bodies to face the document camera, reading the text out loud, scooping up phrases.

LINK

Add the new strategy to your anchor chart, reminding students of the power of rereading.

"Remember, readers, to make your reading voice just as smooth as your singing voice by reading in longer phrases. You can scoop up more words at a time by noticing the punctuation." I added the new strategy Post-it to the chart.

ANCHOR CHART

Making Your Reading More Fluent

- Reread aloud and in your head.
- **Scoop words into longer phrases.**

Scoop words into longer phrases.

Check that it makes sense sounds right.

The words will sound smoother.

Use punctuation.

"Then, you can check that your reading makes sense and sounds right. But that's not all, you know! Remember, also, the power of *rereading*." I tapped the first bullet on the chart. "You can practice a bit out loud, to make your silent reading voice sound just as smooth."

As students are reading and scooping up words into phrases, remember that there is not one right way to phrase the text, and remind students of this as well. Children might chunk the text differently, yet still maintain meaning and syntax. For example, one might read, "... and sit down to write/another chapter in her book," while another reads, "... and sit down/to write another chapter/in her book." As you coach students, make sure that they read in ways that maintain the meaning of the text. You might also share with students examples of different ways to chunk the same passage that work well and others that don't.

CONFERRING AND SMALL-GROUP WORK

Identifying and Helping Readers Who Struggle with Fluency

WHEN CONFERRING TODAY, aim to identify and work with children who have challenges reading with phrasing and fluency. You can help children read with more fluency by providing a lot of modeling. You can read a passage aloud with phrasing and help students see the parts you're reading in a swoop by sliding your finger under each phrase as you say it. This skill does not come easily, so be prepared to practice this for several days.

Help students who are still pointing as they read transition to reading with their eyes only.

Check to see if some kids are still pointing with a finger under each word, because by the time kids are reading level H, they generally shouldn't need to point (though they can bring the finger back for a word that poses word-solving difficulty). Prompt children who still read with their fingers (and are beyond those early stages of reading) to use their eyes, as the eyes move faster than the finger. It's important to help these readers group words together into meaningful parts to increase their fluency and comprehension.

Work with readers who are fast, but need support reading with fluency.

If you have students who read quickly but without phrasing, slow them down and ask them to listen to their own reading to hear whether it sounds like talking. Demonstrate what phrased reading sounds like. If you want to go a step further, you could lay a clear sheet protector over a passage in their text, and as you demonstrate reading the text, draw a line to represent where you pause while reading.

Then, turn the task over to the child and have him note where he pauses. Emphasize that the child should say the words aloud first, and only then mark where a natural pause occurs. Do not expect responses to sound just one way. Welcome approximations, encouraging any evidence that the reader is pausing and beginning to sound phrased and fluent. Perhaps the student will try marking and reading a few lines of text. Then you might say, "Now try reading in phrases without actually making a mark."

Figure out ways to help readers who struggle with fluency.

It's helpful to keep Reading Recovery founder Marie Clay's voice in your ear as you work with young readers. She'll whisper to you that prompting kids to "read it faster" is a very generic prompt, and that figuring out what specifically is keeping a child from doing that can help you support his progress. Is it that the youngster needs a bigger bank of high-frequency words? That he rereads multiple times within just a single sentence, checking constantly? If you note a child who needs to increase his or her fluency, go the extra step and ask yourself, "Why might that be?"

Remember also that texts teach, just as you teach. If a child is struggling to read with fluency, she needs to practice reading books that are easy for her. Reduce the level of challenge—for now. Look, too, at whether a book contains longer sentences, which is preferable for practicing phrasing. Some books are full of extremely short sentences, and they won't be ideal for the purpose of improving fluency.

Finally, when you coach a child's reading, remember to keep your teaching to a minimum. Make sure your prompts are lean and brief and use similar prompts often.

MID-WORKSHOP TEACHING
Checking that Your Reading Makes Sense and Sounds Right

"I want to remind you that a little bit of out-loud reading helps change that in-your-head voice. So, as you're reading, remember to check that the scoops you're making as you read make sense and sound right. You can take out that pretend conch shell and *reread* into it. Whisper read to yourself to check. Ask, 'Does that make sense? Does that sound right?' If not, scoop a different way. Use punctuation to help you. Then, you can go back to silent reading and read on with that same smooth voice."

SHARE

Partners Read to Each Other

Recruit partners to reread together, scooping words in longer, meaningful phrases as they read aloud.

"Readers, you don't need to come to the meeting area for our share today, because the really important thing is that you share with your partners. Choose one book that you especially want to share with your partner, and choose a passage in that book that you want to reread aloud. Then get ready to read it, scooping up the words that help your partner understand what's happening, making sure your phrases make sense and sound right. Practice a bit on your own, first." I gave children time to prepare.

I introduced a new anchor chart for partners and added the first strategy:

ANCHOR CHART

Partners Reread Together to . . .

- **Practice out loud and try to picture what's happening.**

Then I said, "Now huddle up beside your partner and reread to one another. Partner 1, you'll start today. Partner 2, be sure to listen closely to check that you can really picture what's happening and that it sounds right. Then, you might even reread together, working to make your voices even smoother." I moved across the room, listening in as partners read aloud, coaching them to listen and check syntax, asking, "Does that sound right? Reread and try it another way." After a few minutes, I prompted partners to switch roles.

Partners Reread Together to...

Practice out loud and try to picture what's happening.

SESSION 2: SCOOPING UP WORDS INTO PHRASES

Session 3

Noticing Dialogue Tags

IN THIS SESSION, you'll teach children that dialogue tags can help readers read dialogue with expression.

GETTING READY

- Use sentence strips to write dialogue and dialogue tags (see Teaching).
- Read aloud pages 2–5 from *Houndsley and Catina* prior to the minilesson. Project these pages, perhaps using a document camera, and prepare highlighter tape to mark dialogue tags (see Active Engagement).
- Display the anchor chart titled "Making Your Reading More Fluent" and prepare to add the strategy Post-it—"Talk like the characters" (see Link).
- Reveal chart paper with a small passage for students to read (see Mid-Workshop Teaching).
- Display the anchor chart titled "Partners Reread Together to . . ." so that it is ready to refer to, and prepare to add the strategy—"Perform! Bring characters to life." (see Share).

MINILESSON

CONNECTION

Remind students of the work they did around fluency in the last unit.

"Remember in our last unit, when you worked to read your nonfiction books in such a way that your voices matched what the book was trying to teach? You've been working hard to think about what your voice should sound like, so that right from the start, you let the voice of the text come through. Right now, will you think of one idea you have for how you can make your reading sound *even* better?" I gave a moment of silence, using that time to do this thinking myself.

"Turn and talk!" I said, with urgency, as if I knew they'd be like shaken soda bottles, ready to burst with ideas. I listened briefly to a few partnerships, assessing what students knew to say about reading with more fluency. After just a minute, I said, "Oh my gosh! You know a lot about this. You reminded me that reading aloud well means making the characters *talk*—absolutely! The cool thing is that scientists who study readers say the exact same thing!"

Name the teaching point.

"Today I want to teach you that when you are reading dialogue, it is important to be able to hear what it sounds like when the character talks. The dialogue tags tell you not only who is talking, but they also sometimes help you know how the character sounds."

TEACHING

Use prewritten sentence strips and cut-out dialogue tags to practice the work of reading dialogue with varied intonation.

As children joined me in the meeting area, I put a few sentence strips in a pocket chart, with a simple line of dialogue written across each. "You might be wondering what these are," I said, noting that the kids had begun reading the lines to themselves. "I thought we could play a little game together. What do you think?" The class cheered, always ready for a new game.

"Great! Here's how it works. I've written a few different lines of dialogue on each sentence strip. You'll read a line, and then I'll choose a tag to add on. That means, I'll decide *how* it should sound. Then, you'll have a turn to add a dialogue tag. Let's try one together first." I pointed to the first sentence strip, inviting the class to read it aloud with me:

"We are going to the beach today?"

The children read with pleasant, upbeat voices. "Now what would happen if I add this dialogue tag? How would your voices change?" I added a sentence strip, on which I had written, "he whined."

"Oh! That's going to make it different. Whining means he's upset," one voice piped up.

"That's true. Will you reread it the way it should sound?" The class reread the line, adding a bit of dread to their voices.

"Now try again with this tag." I replaced "he whined" with "he said in complete shock." Again, the class reread with different intonation, some wide-eyed, to show the feeling. "Do you see how just one line of talking can sound so differently, depending on how the character is feeling? Dialogue tags help you know how it should sound so your voice matches the character's."

ACTIVE ENGAGEMENT

Channel children to try reading aloud a passage from the class read-aloud text, noting not only *what* the characters say, but also *how* they say it.

"Dialogue tags are all over your books, too. They can help you read your books so that you sound like the characters. Will you and your partner read this short passage from our read-aloud book? Remember to really pay attention not only to *what* the characters are saying, but also to *how* the characters are speaking. Ready to try?" I gestured to the text projected with the document camera.

"When we left off reading the start of *Houndsley and Catina*, the characters were talking about how Catina wanted Houndsley to read her writing," I reminded students, referencing the chapter we had read during read-aloud. "Now, read this passage with your partner, keeping in mind what is going on in the whole story, so you read the dialogue like

Noticing dialogue tags will not only improve students' fluency, but also their understanding of the characters in their books. Dialogue tags, which give clues to what the character is feeling and thinking, help students develop ideas about the characters.

it would actually sound if you heard the characters speaking." I listened in as children read the passage to each other, coaching them to consider how each character was feeling and using dialogue tags to cue intonation.

> "I did not ask if your book was going to win prizes," Houndsley said in his soft-as-a-rose-petal voice. "I asked how the writing was going."
>
> "I will be famous," Catina went on as if she had not heard him.
>
> Houndsley sighed. "May I read your book?" he asked.
>
> "Of course," said Catina. "I have only one chapter left to write."
>
> The next evening, Catina invited Houndsley to her house.
>
> "Here is my book," she said proudly. She gave him all seventy-four chapters, a cup of ginger tea, and a plate of cookies.
>
> "I will need more cookies," said Houndsley.

Rewind the read-aloud the kids just did, this time problematizing key parts and engaging in some interpretive discussion about them.

"Readers, can we rewind to the part when Houndsley goes to Catina's house?" I pointed to the line. "I'll be Catina. Who will be my narrator?"

Emma's hand shot up. "I will."

I nodded and said, "Great, try it." Pointing at the text, Emma read the narration that preceded Catina's line:

> The next evening, Catina invited Houndsley to her house.

I piped up, reading the next line with a somewhat flat voice:

> "Here is my book."

Looking at the other children, I asked them to weigh in. "Do you agree with my way of reading that line? Who might have a different way that line might sound?" The children pointed out that the text said that Catina spoke *proudly*. I highlighted the dialogue tag. They added, "Catina is very proud of her book. She sounds very sure of herself. She is excited about the book." Then, I invited Emma to read the text instead of me, coaching her to make her voice loud and proud, which she did.

We then moved on to role-play Houndsley's line, after discussing that he was expected to read seventy-four chapters (!) of his friend's book.

> "I will need more cookies."

FIG. 3–1   Casey marking dialogue tags

Many of the children thought he'd say that in an exhausted way, and we noted that the text never came out and said that. They knew it from picturing how thick Catina's book must be, widening their own eyes as they imagined the sight of it.

LINK

Send readers off, reminding them that as they read today, they can work on making the dialogue sound right, supplying the intonation that fits with the story.

"Readers, as you go off today, remember that when you are reading dialogue, it is important to be able to hear what it sounds like when the character talks. You can use dialogue tags to help you sound like the character. If you think about the characters and about what's going on in a story, you can picture what the character is doing and understand how the character must be feeling. Then you can reread to make your voice show that."

Remind students that practicing a bit aloud can help them to read silently with equal fluency.

"And don't forget, a little bit of out-loud reading helps your silent reading voice." I gestured toward the first bullet on the chart. "Today, you might start reading aloud to yourself, into your conch. Then, keep on reading the next pages silently, but make sure to still listen to what that reading voice sounds like. If it starts to sound bumpy and boring, reread a bit out loud again before going back to silent reading." I added the new strategy Post-it to the chart.

FIG. 3–2 Henrique marking dialogue tags in Spanish

> **ANCHOR CHART**
>
> Making Your Reading More Fluent
> - Reread aloud and in your head.
> - Scoop words into longer phrases.
> - **Talk like the characters.**
>
> Talk like the characters.

I prompted children to quickly fill out their reading logs and get started with their reading.

CONFERRING AND SMALL-GROUP WORK

Quick Conferences Reinforce Prior Learning

AS YOU CONFER TODAY, continue to conduct some quick individual and table conferences. Some of these conferences may focus on reinforcing the behaviors and skills taught in previous units. It has likely been a few weeks since students read lots of fiction, and they may need to be reminded of strategies from Unit 1. You may be coaching students to get ready to read by giving their texts a quick sneak peek. If children don't do this, act astonished. How could they forget that this is what readers do? Also notice what children do when they come to tricky words. You are apt to see some of them mumble past those words. Again, act astonished. A later bend of this unit focuses on language, but you needn't wait until then to remind readers that when they are unsure of what a word means, they should return to that word after they have read past it and try to figure it out. Above all, be sure that readers are monitoring for sense. If they read something and it's clear it won't make sense, and yet you don't see the reader thinking "Huh?" and returning to reread using fix-up strategies, show them that you can't imagine how a reader in your class could just read on, whether or not the book makes sense.

It's also important to be ready to celebrate the brilliant things readers do. If you see someone working to figure out a tricky word, make a big fuss about it. "You aren't the kind of reader who just says, 'Oh well, who cares?' No way! You know that figuring out words is part of reading, and you're willing to do whatever it takes to make sure that book makes sense! Great job!"

Assess and scaffold fluency.

As you confer today and throughout the unit, you can continue to collect data around fluency. Asking students to begin today by reading aloud provides an opportunity to circulate among kids, checking on whether their read-aloud voices sound like their speaking voices.

You may find that some students are reading much too fast, racing past punctuation cues mid-sentence, as well as end punctuation. This will often result in readers not

---

MID-WORKSHOP TEACHING
Who's Talking? Keeping Track of Dialogue

"Readers, some of you are finding that the dialogue can sometimes be tricky to track! What I mean is, it's not always easy to figure out *who* is talking. You see, your books don't always include a dialogue tag. Sometimes just the words are there, but not who said them, or even how they were said. Have you noticed that? It might go like this . . ." I projected a sample snippet of dialogue I had written, including two lines with tags and two without.

> *"Hi," said Jack.*
> *"How's it going?" said Jill.*
> *"Good!"*
> *"Me, too."*

"Thumbs up if you've seen dialogue in your books like this." Many children acknowledged they had. "Well when that happens, you are supposed to read it, adding in those tags yourself in your head: 'said A' and 'said B.' Like this . . ." I reread the snippet, this time emphasizing how I assigned each line of untagged dialogue to a speaker.

> *"Hi," said Jack.*
> *"How's it going?" said Jill.*
> *"Good!"* **said Jack**.
> *"Me, too,"* **said Jill**.

"So be on the lookout for dialogue like this so you can be sure to add in who said what in your head to help you keep track. Keep reading!"

phrasing properly, as they rush through words across the page. Coach these readers to slow down, attending to punctuation to prompt pauses in the reading. You might coach a reader to scan the page before reading, previewing the punctuation she'll encounter as she reads. You might even have the child use small pieces of highlighter tape to flag punctuation before reading. This is, of course, a scaffold you'll quickly remove, but it may serve to engage students in the work of noticing punctuation as a way to support stronger fluency.

You may also choose to support students with phrasing and intonation by echo reading. Play the role of a proficient partner, reading aloud one sentence at a time to demonstrate how to break the sentence into meaningful chunks. Prosodic phrasing is a characteristic that's universal across all languages. Teach readers to listen to themselves read to monitor for meaning and syntax, thinking, "Did that make sense and sound right? How would I say that if I were talking?" Coach students as they read aloud, supporting their ability to match their reading voices to the phrasing and intonation they use in spoken language.

You can also support fluency by tapping into the power of rereading. You might pull a small group to engage in multiple readings of a short text, such as lyrics to a popular song, an engaging poem, or an excerpt of a longer text, such as a page from a familiar read-aloud. As texts grow more and more familiar, students will undoubtedly become more fluent readers of that text, as well as developing into more fluent readers of unfamiliar texts.

SHARE

Readers Reread to Make Their Voices Smooth and Expressive

Suggest that partners perform scenes together, rereading passages from their books to bring characters to life, using expressive voices and gestures.

"Your reading voices are getting smoother with every sentence you read. And you know that rereading helps you become smoother, more fluent readers. Partners help, too. Yesterday, you worked together to read aloud in ways that helped you actually picture what was happening on the page. Today I want to add that you can bring those parts to life! You can reread to perform scenes in your book, pretending to be different characters and using gestures to show their actions and feelings." I added another strategy to the partner chart:

> **ANCHOR CHART**
>
> Partners Reread Together to . . .
> - Practice out loud and try to picture what's happening.
> - **Perform! Bring characters to life.**

Entice partners to reread scenes from their books, comparing this work to the rereading actors do to prepare for a movie.

"Right now, quickly find a scene or two from your book that would be fun to perform. It should probably be a part that has a lot of dialogue." I gave partners a moment to locate a few passages. "Mark those parts with a Post-it and get together with your partner to do some rereading, *ahem*, or should I say *rehearsing*. After all, movie stars are the biggest rereaders of all! They need to read and reread their lines many ways to get their voices to sound exactly right. So spend the rest of our workshop time rereading scenes together, pretending to be different characters in the book, using your reading voices to bring those characters to life."

Session 4

Using Meaning to Read Fluently

MINILESSON

CONNECTION

Gather children to the meeting area, creating noticeable changes in your tone of voice as you do so.

"Come to the rug," I said in an unusually brash tone. Students sensed the urgency in my voice and came to the rug quickly, with some trepidation. "Good morning readers," I said in a kind tone, and watched as the children responded with smiles spread across their faces.

"Readers, did you see how I used two different voices there? When I wanted you to come quickly to the rug, I used an authoritative tone of voice. When you heard that tone, you immediately knew I meant business and came to the rug. Then, when I said, 'Good morning,' I was using my usual kind, sweet voice, and you relaxed.

"I'm telling you this because readers need to study the way that authors indicate the appropriate tone of voice to use when reading a text. Yesterday, you studied the way this one cue (and I drew a quote mark) can affect how you read a text. Today, you'll study other ways that authors let readers know how to read a text."

❖ **Name the teaching point.**

"Today I want to teach you that to read a book—even in your head—and to make it sound right, you have to consider what it's about. If you're telling your best friend bad news, your voice will sound different than if you're telling that friend about winning first place in a contest. When you know what the text is about, you can show that with your voice."

IN THIS SESSION, you'll teach children that readers match their voices to the meaning of the text.

GETTING READY

- Reveal chart paper with a small passage for students to read (see Teaching).
- Prepare to read pages 22–24 from *Houndsley and Catina* or another similar demonstration text (see Active Engagement).
- Display the anchor chart titled "Making Your Reading More Fluent" so that it is ready to refer to, and add the strategy Post-it—"Make your voice match the mood." (see Link and Share).

TEACHING

Point out that reading at this level involves more than figuring out the words. Demonstrate how readers often figure out intonation and meaning from context.

"Readers, when you were younger, reading meant figuring out the words on the page and saying them. But as you get older, reading means figuring out not only the words, but the actions, interactions, moods, and gestures that bring the text to life. Some of that will be spelled out by the author, but much of it requires knowing what is going on in the story. For example, read this . . ." and I pointed to a piece of chart paper on which I'd written one word: *no*. The children read the word aloud.

Leaning forward, I said, "Now, think about *how* you read that. What did your intonation suggest you meant?" I asked, knowing they wouldn't understand me yet. "Try reading that same word—*no*—again, but this time, you'll know more about how to read the word because it will come in the middle of a larger text." I revealed a small passage. "Read this word with your partner, trying to figure out how the text wants you to read that two-letter word, whenever it comes." I then read the passage aloud, leaving spaces for the kids to read the word *no* with the inflection called for by the context.

> *My dad got my brother and me tickets to a fancy circus. My brother wasn't that excited. He said, "I don't think I'm going to go." My dad looked him in the eyes and said, "No? Really?"*
>
> *My brother looked unsure. He seemed to consider going to the circus after all. Then he shook his head and said . . .*

I paused, pointing to Diana to fill in the word *no*, which she produced in a whiny voice: "*Noooo.*"

Then we read on together, and again, I left a space for children to read the next few *no's* with meaningful intonation.

> *I wasn't sure he meant it. Checking, I asked, "No?"*

"Nice work using what's happening in the text to help you figure out how to read it this time around. You may have noticed the question mark as a clue. You were correct to change your voice—there's uncertainty in the story, and you made your voices match that."

> *He signaled that he was definite.*
>
> *I repeated what I'd learned. It was final.* No.

"Thumbs up if there were some words here that gave you clues for how to read this word." Several students gave a thumbs up. "Thumbs up if you read the word *definite*, and that helped you match your voice to what was happening. How about *final*? Nice work. When you pay attention to what's really happening, it helps you read with more expression. Keep going."

Notice that this minilesson requires you to exaggerate with contrasting tones, and later reflect back on the different voices you used. Don't be subtle.

At this point, you may want to reread the sentence and supply intonation for the word no *so that kids grasp what you are expecting. You may find that when the whole class choral reads the word* no, *intonation gets lost in the wash. In that case, as you continue reading the passage, point like a conductor in a symphony to one person only to say the word* no *with appropriate intonation.*

My Dad nodded. He was fine about it. "Then no it is," he said, smiling broadly. The dog approached, and tried to climb onto my Dad's lap. He pushed the dog down firmly. "No," he said, and the dog left the room.

Debrief, emphasizing the transferable point that context offers helpful clues about appropriate intonation, talking in ways that apply to any text, any day.

"Did you hear how you had to fill in the *no* with different voices each time, even when the word looked exactly the same?" The kids nodded. "Readers, my point is that you need to understand what is going on in a story to be able to read in ways that show the full meaning. And fluent readers notice not only *what* is being said, but *how* the author is telling you to read it."

ACTIVE ENGAGEMENT

Recruit partners to examine the mood of the text, reading and rereading to make their voices match.

"Are you ready to try this with a partner? As you read together, try and make your voice match how the author wants you to read it. Look for clues in the story to help you. I'll give you a minute to try and think about it with your partner, and then we will hear an example."

I used the document camera to show pages 22–24 of *Houndsley and Catina*, our demonstration text.

> *Houndsley had made his three-bean chili many times before, but today everything went wrong.*
>
> *He dropped a can of tomatoes on his foot.*
>
> *He did not cook the rice long enough.*
>
> *And he forgot to put in the beans. All three kinds!*
>
> *When the judges came to taste his chili, they made faces.*

"Boys and girls, together with your partners, read and reread this part, making your voices match the mood of the text," I said, as I got off my chair to coach individual partnerships.

After coaching a few partnerships, I brought everyone back and selected one partnership to show the class their efforts. "Maddie and Brian are going to show you how they read this part. Get your thumbs ready and see if you think their voices match the mood."

After Maddie and Brian read the passage with an upset or worried tone, many students had their thumbs up. "Wow, I see that many of you agree with Maddie and Brian. Why do you agree? Quickly, whisper to your partner why you agree, using details from the text to help you explain." After a few moments, I gathered the students back and said, "I heard

In supporting partnerships today, you may use lean coaching prompts as students practice the work. You may say things like, "Reread it again, the way you think it sounds best," or "Use key words and phrases to help you figure out how to say it."

SESSION 4: USING MEANING TO READ FLUENTLY

many of you say, 'Everything went wrong.' Great! You were able to match your reading voice with the text and to look for words or phrases that carry the meaning of the story to help you figure out how it should sound."

LINK

Remind children of the repertoire of ways they've learned to make their reading sound more fluent, and encourage them to apply those strategies to their independent reading.

"Readers, as you go off to read today, let's remember what we are learning from research scientists to help you improve and make your reading more fluent." I took out the chart, pointed to the heading, and began to read. I added the next strategy Post-it—"Make your voice match the mood."

ANCHOR CHART

Making Your Reading More Fluent

- Reread aloud and in your head.
- Scoop words into longer phrases.
- Talk like the characters.
- **Make your voice match the mood.**

Make your voice match the mood.

"So, your work as readers isn't *just* to read. No! It's to *improve* your reading by trying to make it sound even better, even when you are reading it silently in your mind. You may want to think to yourself as you read, 'Does my voice sound like what the story is trying to show? Does my voice match the mood?'"

CONFERRING AND SMALL-GROUP WORK

Approaching Reading Workshop with Students' Data in Mind

YOU'LL APPROACH READING WORKSHOP TIME with different plans for readers who are working at different levels of text complexity. Those who are reading at benchmark levels (K or L) will be reading books like *Frog and Toad* by Arnold Lobel or *Slinky Scaly Snakes* by Jennifer Dussling. Plan to help these students ramp up their reading volume as well as their fluency (which should be well supported in the unit), as the books they're encountering will be longer than any they have read prior to now. Typically, their books may be around sixty to ninety pages long. This means that they'll be reading a story over multiple days, so you may need to remind them to recall where they are in a storyline by looking back over the text before they begin the day's reading.

Other students will be reading below benchmark level. Review your data on these students and think carefully about what it shows to understand what will help them most. If some of these students need support with fluency, one potent way to support them is to do some small-group shared reading. You could say, "Readers, we are going to do some shared reading together. We read this book as a class, but I was thinking we could reread it in a small group. This will give you a chance to work on the speed—or the pace, as some people call it—of your reading, because I've noticed that you/often/read/a/bit/slowly. By rereading this together, we can all practice reading a bit more quickly."

Of course, after you work with these readers on a shared text, while they are still sitting together in a small group, you can ask them to pull a book from their baggies and read it with the same pace and fluency as they used to reread the shared reading book with your support.

> **MID-WORKSHOP TEACHING** **Readers Picture What's Happening, Then Make Their Voices Match**
>
> "Readers, can I please have your eyes and ears?" I waited for the students to lift their gaze and look at me standing in the middle of the classroom. "Readers, reading researchers have found that when you picture what is happening in a text, that can help you read it like a master storyteller.
>
> "So, if you are reading a story, really try and picture the character and think about what she's doing and how she's doing it. If you are reading about someone in a hailstorm, really picture the hail—little golf-ball-sized chunks of ice—pounding into things like cars and bicycles. *Ouch*!" I held a hand to the top of my head as if hit by a hailstone.
>
> "As you picture what's happening and what things look like and even feel like, use your voice to help bring the scene to life! Picturing something in your mind helps to improve your reading—both how you sound and how well you understand!
>
> "Try it, right now. Look back in your book at a part you can reread, getting the clearest picture you can of what's happening. Now, see if the voice out loud and in your head gets better. Then read on, trying the same thing again!"

SESSION 4: USING MEANING TO READ FLUENTLY

SHARE

Researching Fluency and Giving Tips

"Readers, will you bring your book baggies and come to the meeting, sitting next to your partner?" As soon as the students were settled, I said, "You have been learning about what research scientists say about reading, and today, I thought you could do a little research for yourselves. Would *you* like to become reading researchers?" The kids chimed in, saying they would.

"Right now, one partner is the reader, and one partner is the reading researcher. Then you'll switch. Reading researchers, get ready to really research your reader and notice all the ways she has been working to make her reading more fluent. Can you give your reader feedback using hand signals—a thumbs up, or not-so-sure (wobbly thumb)? Remember, you can use the chart to help you think about what to research. If you want, ask your reader to reread, trying to make it smoother or faster." I referenced the anchor chart.

After children worked on this for a bit, I asked them to switch roles. "Listen and check if the reader's voice matches the character's. Then, give some tips."

I listened as students continued this work. I heard Jeremiah say, "That doesn't sound like the character." I knelt down beside Jeremiah and whispered to him, "It'd be better to help. What would help? Give a tip!" Jeremiah paused and then said, "Read it with more excitement." I continued to move around, listening to partners work and coaching as needed.

Session 5

Reading at a Just-Right Pace

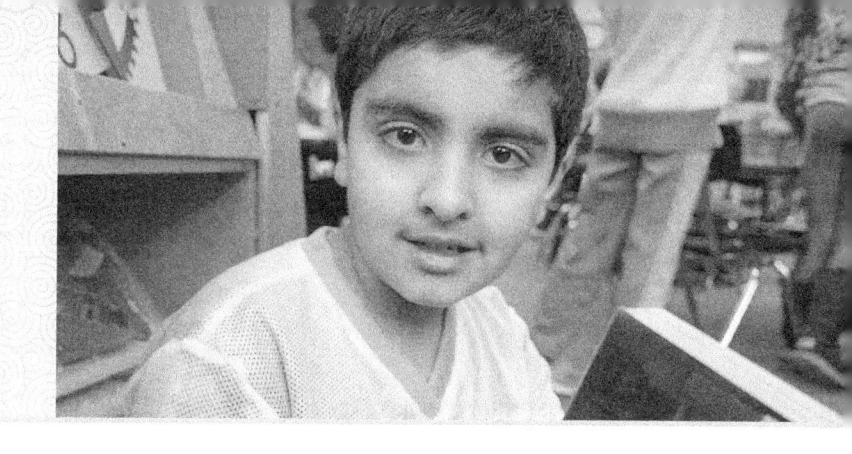

IN THIS SESSION, you'll teach students that readers make sure they read at a pace that is not too fast and not too slow—one that allows them to understand what they are reading.

MINILESSON

CONNECTION

Rally students to understand the importance of finding their just-right reading pace.

"How many of you remember the story of 'Goldilocks and the Three Bears'?" I asked. "Remember how she kept testing different things out until she found what was just right for her? Her story makes me think of you, and how, as second-graders, you are figuring out your just-right reading pace.

"Sometimes, you try reading a book, and . . ." I quickened my voice to spit out the next few words quickly, "you read it way too fast!"

I altered my voice to make it much more drawn-out. "Then . . . you . . . try . . . reading it . . . and . . . you read it . . ."

"Too slow!" the students shouted out.

I steadied my voice. "Exactly right. But *then*, you listen to yourself and you think, 'Wait! I want to read this so it makes sense and sounds good, out loud and in my head,' and you read it . . ."

"Just right!"

"Yes! A just-right reading pace isn't about speeding through, nor is it like just moseying along! It feels normal, like you are understanding the book and hearing it clearly in your mind. It sounds like you're having a conversation with someone."

GETTING READY

- Prepare to read pages 29–30 of *Houndsley and Catina* or a similar demonstration text that you have chosen (see Teaching).
- Display the anchor chart "Making Your Reading More Fluent" so it is ready to refer to, and add the strategy Post-it—"Read with a just-right pace." (see Link).
- Display *Houndsley and Catina* to the class (see Active Engagement).
- Prepare for students to review their reading logs (see Mid-Workshop Teaching).

❖ **Name the teaching point.**

"Today I want to teach you that reading a story so it can be understood doesn't just require intonation and expression; it also requires that you adjust your speed. If you go too fast, your words/all/blur/together, and . . . if . . . you . . . go . . . too . . . slow, it's hard to make sense of the text. Readers learn to adjust their speed so it's just right."

TEACHING

Explain what a just-right reading pace should feel and sound like.

"When readers read too *s-l-o-w-l-y*, they often have trouble *remembering* the whole story—they forget what happened in the beginning by the time they get to the end! Whoa! That's a big problem. Thumbs up if sometimes that happens to you." A few honest thumbs went up.

"And when readers read too *fast*, they often miss important parts because they race right past words, so they don't understand everything they've read. Does that sometimes happen to some of you?" A few more children nodded. "Did you know that *second* grade is *the* most important year to improve upon your pace? Well, when I heard that, I jumped right out of my chair. Second grade? That's you, right now! You have the chance right now to read, not too fast and not too slow, *but* just right! That way, you'll understand everything you read even better!"

Demonstrate reading an excerpt in search of your just-right reading pace.

"Readers, watch me try and find my just-right pace. I am going to pretend to be a second-grader who needs to work on this. Are you ready to watch me try?" I asked. I began to read an excerpt from *Houndsley and Catina*, starting on page 29.

I showed the text using the document camera and began to read aloud in a slow and choppy voice, pointing under each word.

> *One night, Houndsley and Catina were sitting . . .*

"You saw and heard how choppy that was with my finger, right? I'm going to take my finger away and really move my eyes across the page. See if you can move your eyes to keep up with my voice." I reread the sentence from the beginning to the end.

"Sounded better right? Not too slow. I sped it up a bit, really trying to push my eyes across the words. Keep watching, I'm going to do the next bit now. Listen and watch." My reading of the next sentence was fast and furious and incomprehensible.

> *This was one of their favorite things to do together.*

Tim Rasinski's research suggests that students who read above the recommended words per minute often miss things or lose details. Students who read slower than the recommendation have a hard time remembering the beginning of the book when they get to the end. Students who read at the recommended reading rate of 75–100 words per minute at the end of second grade have the highest comprehension.

"Way too fast, right? Now I'm going to slow down and scoop up smaller bits and add a little expression to my voice. Read along with me, in your mind, and see if our voices match!" I reread the sentence with better phrasing and a bit of stress on the word *favorite*.

"Better right? Not too fast and not too slow, but . . ."

"*Just right*!"

"Did you see how I am not trying to rush past the words, nor am I just letting my voice sag and meander slowly? I am trying to pick up my pace and sound like a storyteller. To do that, sometimes you need to speed up, and sometimes you need to slow down. You need to use *all* the things you know to help you read like a storyteller!"

I asked students to give me a thumbs up if I read the next sentence with a just-right pace. Up they went.

ACTIVE ENGAGEMENT

Recruit students to read the next passage aloud, working on their just-right reading pace. Then, guide partners to assess reading speed and offer the reader a tip.

"Readers, now it's your turn to try with me." I showed the next part of *Houndsley and Catina* with the document camera. "All the Partner 1s, will you go first and read this passage aloud?"

"Everyone—but especially the Partner 2s—think about the pace. Does it sound too fast, too slow, or . . . just right? Then you can give a tip, like, 'Pick up the speed. Push your eyes across the page!' Or 'Slow it down. Scoop up a few words and show more expression!' Or, 'Don't forget the punctuation!' Are you ready? Let's read!"

> At last, Houndsley said, "I did not need a new set of pots and pans.
>
> I only wanted to win that contest to show everyone I was the best cook."

"Partner 2s, what do you think? Too fast, too slow, or just right?"

"Too slow!" they all sang out in unison!

"Give your Partner 1 a tip then!"

"Okay, let's pick up the speed. Let's push our eyes across the page. I'll run the pointer quickly under the words. Keep your voice up with mine!" We reread the text with much better fluency.

"Partner 2s, do we get the just-right pace thumbs up? I think so too! Now let's switch. Partner 2s, read. Everyone think about the pace. Partner 1s, get ready to give us a tip!"

SESSION 5: READING AT A JUST-RIGHT PACE

It's important to emphasize that finding a just-right reading pace is not a speed contest. Many students will speed through books without monitoring for meaning.

You may decide to list some of these tips for improving reading rate on a chart: pick up speed, push your eyes across the page, slow down, scoop up the words in phrases, show more expression, don't forget the punctuation. However, you may instead decide to encourage your students to give each other whatever tips come to mind, using what they already know about smooth, expressive, fluent reading.

"You are the best cook," Catina said.

"I do not need to be the best," said Houndsley in his soft-as-a-rose-petal voice.

"Well . . . ?"

"Too slow!"

"Again! Yep, I agree. Partner 1, tell Partner 2 what could help!"

"Let's reread it again and kick up the speed! Get those eyes sweeping across the words. Make your voices sound like the characters." We reread again with greater fluency.

"Wow, readers, with just a little practice thinking about your pace, you were able to adjust your reading speed. Thinking about the pace and kicking it up a notch helped you read it in the way that the author, James Howe, probably wanted it to sound! Doesn't this help you understand so much better what he is trying to say?"

LINK

Remind students of all of the strategies they have learned to help them read fluently, emphasizing reading at a just-right pace.

"Whenever you are reading, whether out loud or in your head, make sure that you understand what is happening and that your voice sounds just right. Thinking about and adjusting your *pace* of reading will help you understand the text even better.

"If you read too slowly or too fast, it's easy to miss important parts and harder to remember what's happening in your book. Good luck today in finding your own just-right reading pace. You can do it! Remember all the things we have been doing to become more fluent. Doing *all* these things as you read will help!" I pointed to the anchor chart.

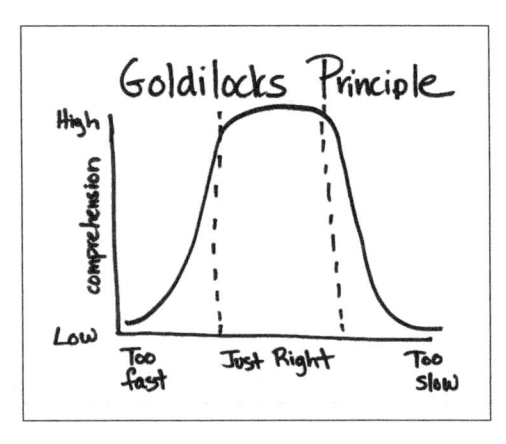

FIG. 5–1 The Goldilocks principle can help readers find their just-right pace.

ANCHOR CHART

Making Your Reading More Fluent

- Reread aloud and in your head.
- Scoop words into longer phrases.
- Talk like the characters.
- Make your voice match the mood.
- **Read with a just-right pace.**

CONFERRING AND SMALL-GROUP WORK

Checking In on Pace and Comprehension

IT'S USEFUL to consult students' reading logs and listen to them read to evaluate how they are doing with pace. In some cases, students may be spending several days on a level K or L book, which could mean they are not doing the volume of reading needed to move up levels. It could be a sign that it's not a just-right text, and they may be reading books above their independent reading level. You may want to check to see if this is the case and make sure students are reading books independently at a level that's just right for them. There may also be a group of students flying through books at a very fast pace. This could be a problem, as they are not really reading to understand their stories. You could pull a group of students that struggle with this, perhaps using the "Goldilocks principle" diagram (pictured in Figure 5–1). When students improve their pace, their reading comprehension should improve. You can encourage them to practice reading and rereading until they can feel what a just-right pace sounds like. Around the K and L level, that may be around ninety words per minute.

Support readers in using the strategies you are teaching them throughout the day.

Make sure that children have opportunities for repeated practice with strategies across the day. Look for time outside of reading workshop when you can work on things like intonation, pace, and phrasing. For example, you might work on phrasing as you are rehearsing for your class play. During science or social studies, you might have students scoop up words and find phrases in texts, marking them with Wikki Stix. You might read the class schedule or morning message during transitions, inviting the class to chorally read the day's agenda: "After gym, we will go to lunch."

Another great time to practice these skills is during writing workshop. When students are writing, encourage them to reread their pieces out loud. This will help them write with rhythm and flow, as well as practice reading with fluency.

MID-WORKSHOP TEACHING   **Using Reading Logs to Reflect**

Ask students to review their reading logs to assess and reflect on their reading pace.

"Readers, you have been working on your just-right reading pace. One way to check to your just-right reading pace is to look at your reading logs. Take out your log right now, and carefully study it like a reading researcher."

"Readers, you know that your reading logs can really help you track your reading progress. Count how many books you have read this week, and hold that number in your head. Now, think to yourself if you want to try to add one more book to that number for next week's total. You may also think to yourself that your number is high, and maybe you want to read fewer books next week so you can read each one more carefully. At the top of your log, quickly jot down a goal for the number of books you would like to read next week, based on the research you did on your own reading logs."

You can coach students to read a number of books that are appropriate for their levels. J–L readers should be reading about six to eight books per week in school during reading workshop. M readers may read about five to six books in a week. Book totals for the week will be higher if students are reading at home as well.

SESSION 5: READING AT A JUST-RIGHT PACE

SHARE

Putting It All Together to Get . . . a Fluent Reader!

Remind students of all the strategies they have learned about reading fluently by reviewing the chart.

"Readers, you have spent the past several days really working on becoming a fluent reader. You have learned so many ways to make your reading more fluent." I reread the chart with the students.

Channel students to select their favorite part of a book to perform for a fluency celebration. Remind students to reread that part a few times, making sure they are using all their strategies.

"I thought we could have a mini-celebration, a symphony share, where each of you reads out into the circle a favorite part of your book—just a few sentences, not the *whole* book. So go ahead and find a part in your book worth sharing. Pick a couple of sentences, or about half a page, that you will read aloud in the circle. Practice that part, quietly out loud, right now. Try and use *all* of the fluency strategies on the chart as best you can! Try to reread it a few times.

"I will give you just two minutes to practice with your partner. Your partner will listen to see how many things on the chart you are doing. If you are doing all five, you can give your partner a high five! If not, give your partner a tip or a goal for what he should concentrate on to make his reading more fluent."

I walked around the circle, coaching students to reflect on what they were doing, giving them tips, and reminding them to reread.

Then I said, "Let's begin!" Students sat in a circle and began reading their parts out loud when I pointed to them with my pretend baton. After each reader finished, the audience gave silent applause.

Making Your Reading More Fluent

- Reread aloud and in your head.
- Scoop words into longer phrases.
- Talk like the characters.
- Make your voice match the mood.
- Read with a 'just right' pace.

Understanding Literary Language BEND II

Session 6

Recognizing Literary Language

IN THIS SESSION, you'll teach children that readers pay attention to literary language—comparisons, invented words, figurative language—asking, "What might the author want me to see, to understand?"

GETTING READY

- Print the text of the research bulletin to read to students (see Connection).
- Use a familiar read-aloud text with literary language. We suggest *Owl Moon* by Jane Yolen (see Teaching).
- Create a new anchor chart titled "Understanding Literary Language" with all four steps of the first strategy—"Pay attention to special language." "Notice when words are used in special ways." "Reread that part." "Remember what's going on in the story," and "Think, 'What special meaning does the author want me to get?'" (see Teaching and Link).
- Make sure students have Post-its available to mark literary language in their books (Link).
- Place a basket of poetry and books that include comparisons, invented words, and figurative language on each table. Baskets should stay on tables for students to use throughout the bend (see Mid-Workshop Teaching).
- Display the anchor chart from Bend I titled "Partners Reread Together to . . . ," so that it is ready to refer to, and prepare to add the strategy—"Discuss literary language." (see Share).

MINILESSON

CONNECTION

Share a report from reading scientists saying that the books second-graders read often contain playful, inventive language.

"Readers, I have to tell you something. Last night, I got an email blast from the same three reading scientists who told us that second grade is the time when kids start reading silently, and that rereading, especially aloud, helps readers with their in-the-head voices.

"The reading researchers said *again* how important second grade is for growth in reading, but this time they were talking about something a little different. Listen to what they wrote." I pulled out a page and unfolded it dramatically.

> *Research Bulletin about Second-Grade Readers*
>
> *Researchers have found that the books second-graders read often contain language that is used in playful and inventive ways. Second-graders who are especially skilled readers pay attention when a writer has used words in special ways because they know that those passages require extra thought.*

"That was the end of the announcement. I looked for more," I turned the page over as if still looking, "but that was it. So what do we do with this news?" I reread the bulletin.

Share your concern that the class may not have been paying much attention to special uses of language.

"I started thinking about whether we *have* been paying extra attention to passages that use language in playful, inventive ways. Have we been reading right by those passages, not even noticing? I started to worry."

❖ Name the teaching point.

"Today I want to teach you that when authors use language in especially inventive, playful ways, it's kind of like they are pulling on a reader's sleeve saying, 'Notice this!' Skilled readers notice when an author has done something special and think extra hard to make sure they understand what the author is trying to say or show."

TEACHING

Return to the book your students read aloud earlier in the unit, and channel them to notice uses of literary language in a passage you read aloud.

"Readers, earlier, we read aloud parts of Jane Yolen's book *Owl Moon*. We tried to read the book with feeling, picturing the scenes as we read." I read the first few lines to set the scene.

> *It was late one winter night*
>
> *long past my bedtime,*
>
> *when Pa and I went owling.*

"Let's reread a couple parts of that book, and *this* time, if you notice special language—maybe the author compares one thing to another, or makes up words, or uses words in unusual ways—will you point out that she has done something special, something that deserves extra thought? This time, let's *not* just read right past those parts!"

"I'm going to reread from the middle of the book, when Pa and the narrator are deep in the woods." I projected the page with the document camera so students could see the text.

> *We reached the line*
>
> *of pine trees,*
>
> *black and pointy*
>
> *against the sky,*
>
> *and Pa held up his hand.*
>
> *I stopped right where I was*
>
> *and waited.*
>
> *He looked up,*
>
> *as if searching the stars,*
>
> *as if reading a map up there.*

As you read the excerpt, you will want to read the part containing literary language in a way that signals to students that this is the part to pay attention to. If students need additional support, you may decide to point under the literary language. You could even reread those words, and demonstrate as you marvel at them.

SESSION 6: RECOGNIZING LITERARY LANGUAGE

By this point, kids were on their knees, signaling, "Wait, wait!" I pretended to be startled by their interruption. "Oh! Sorry! I almost didn't see you. You noticed something?" I asked.

The kids pointed out that the author had used language in a special way. One reread the description of Pa looking up, "as if searching the stars, as if reading a map up there."

"Good thing you stopped me," I said. "I almost read right past that! Yes, that line deserves our attention!" I reread the sentence.

Explain your process of responding to literary language and unveil a new chart that captures these steps: notice, reread, recall, question.

"To pay attention to special language, I do a few things. First, I notice it. Second, I reread it. Third, I recall what's going on in the story at that point. And fourth, I question what the author is trying to convey with the special language. I ask, 'Why did the author use these particular words? What special meaning does the author want me to get?'"

I unveiled a new chart that captured this process and read it aloud.

ANCHOR CHART

Understanding Literary Language

- Pay attention to special language.
  1. Notice when words are used in special ways.
  2. Reread that part.
  3. Remember what's going on in the story.
  4. Think, "What special meaning does the author want me to get?"

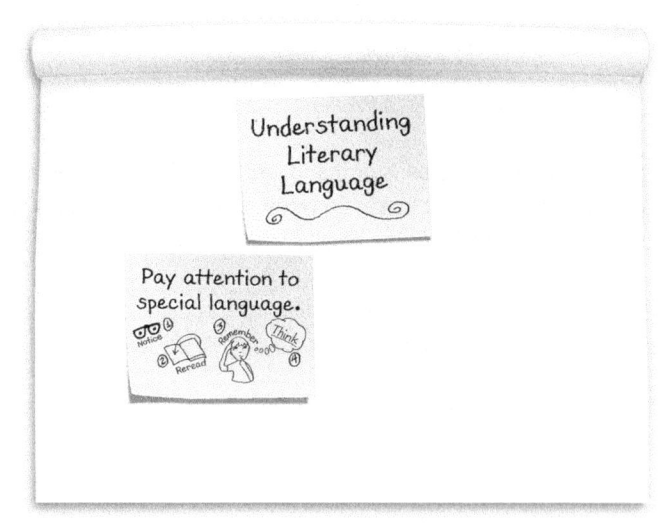

Recruit students to practice this process. Ask them to remember what's happening in the story, and then consider what meaning the author wants to convey with the special language.

"Now, turn and talk with your partner and the partnership next to you about what's going on in the story at this point and think 'What special meaning does the author want me to get?'" The children talked in clusters, recalling that Pa is in the wintery woods, looking for an owl, getting ready to make the call that brings out the owls. "Each of you, without standing up, act out Pa. I'm going to reread this part. Remember to use everything you know from the whole story to act it out. Ready?" I reread the whole passage.

I asked, "So what does it mean that Pa searched the stars as if reading a map up there? What does the author want us to know about how he looked up at the sky? Turn and talk."

The children talked for a minute, and then I said, "I heard many of you say that this comparison shows that Pa was staring really hard at the sky—like you stare at a map. Some of you said that Pa was looking up at the sky because he was trying to find clues about where the owl might be."

Debrief in ways that are transferable to other times and to other texts.

"Remembering what's going on in the whole story is a big part of figuring out what authors mean when they use inventive language," I said. "I love the way you are really thinking, asking, 'What might the author want me to get?' You know the author used words in special ways for a reason, and you're paying attention."

ACTIVE ENGAGEMENT

Channel kids to do the same work with another passage. Read it aloud, and then ask kids to talk about special uses of language, musing over what the author was aiming to say.

"I'm going to read another passage from *Owl Moon*. Will you and your partner do this same sort of thinking without my help?" I pointed to the list of steps they could take, and then read another page of *Owl Moon*.

> *The moon made his face*
>
> *into a silver mask.*
>
> *Then he called:*
>
> *"Whoo-whoo-who-who-who-whooooooo,"*
>
> *the sound of a Great Horned Owl.*

I paused and reread the line, "The moon made his face into a silver mask." Then I prompted partners to discuss this part. "Turn and tell your partner what special language you see here—and what it might mean."

After a minute or two, I gathered the children back together to share their thinking. "Readers, you all know that the moon didn't *really* turn Pa's face into a silver mask. But you noticed that Jane Yolen uses these words in a special way—to create a particular image—and you reread that part carefully. You remembered what's happening in the story; this is the part where Pa first calls out into the night like an owl.

"Then you talked about what special meaning the author was trying to share. Some of you said that maybe Jane Yolen is trying to show how brightly lit Pa's face is, or how big the moon is that night. These are great ideas. This is the type of work readers do to think about why an author chooses certain words."

LINK

Repeat the rallying cry that invigorates this bend of the unit, and the day's teaching point about paying attention to special language.

"Readers, those researchers were right that the books you are reading now use playful, inventive language. Lots of times, the author will use words that you and I know—they aren't new *words*, necessarily—but the author does something special with the words—maybe using them in a new way.

"Today, you got some practice noticing passages where the author has done just that. You gave those passages extra thought so that you would get what the author is trying to say or show." I referenced the new chart again.

"As you go off to read today, you can be on the lookout for places in your books where the author has used language in ways that almost seem to be pulling at your sleeve saying, 'Notice me!' It's a good idea to mark those places with a Post-it and think about them a bit, so that later today, you'll be ready to talk with your partner about them."

CONFERRING AND SMALL-GROUP WORK

Noticing Figurative Language in Other Books

THE START OF A NEW BEND is traditionally a time when your teaching will tend to be more connected to the minilesson than may generally be the case. Typically, you'll devote most of that day's workshop to getting the new work going smoothly, making sure it has traction, at least with the readers for whom the instruction is especially well suited. Once many kids are doing the work of the minilesson, you can rest assured that those early adopters will function as role models for others, and the new work will spread.

Today, therefore, you'll certainly want to help readers throughout your classroom notice instances when authors have used figurative language. Understanding literary language is important for readers who are working in the transitional reading levels and beyond. Texts at beginning reading levels are usually more straightforward. You'll find that the better the writing, the more likely the book will include rich literary language. Among students reading all-star authors, such as Arnold Lobel, William Steig, Cynthia Rylant, Kate DiCamillo, James Howe, Rosemary Wells, or Kevin Henkes, it's likely that if a child says, "This book just has regular language," he merely needs to have his eyes opened to what literary language is.

You might say in a conference, "One thing I do when I want to become the kind of reader who notices literary language—that's what it's called when authors use language in special ways—is reread, trying to pay attention not just to the main events of the story—to who is doing what when. Instead, I try to pay attention to the details that an author includes, and to the particular ways that characters do things. I know the details matter, and the ways things are done matter, too." If you and the child sit reading, side by side, you can demonstrate the sort of quietly responsive reading that you hope the child will do. Just read along, gasping at beautiful lines, whispering a thought as the language strikes you. Then, pass the baton to the child and take a backseat role. This works well in books that are laden with examples of literary language.

Support children who are reading below benchmark level with the work of the bend as well, by drawing their attention to any type of literary language they are encountering.

On the other hand, there will be some books—including most of those written at levels of text complexity below K/L—in which the language tends to be largely literal. You might channel readers at those levels to notice times when the author uses repetition deliberately. Often, a repeated phrase creates cohesion and emphasis. You can coach youngsters to realize that when the author repeats a phrase that was used earlier in the book, each later use of that phrase calls to mind the earlier uses of it, giving that bit of language layers of meaning.

MID-WORKSHOP TEACHING
Don't Let Inventive Language Pass Readers By

Standing in the middle of the room, I said, "Readers, will you make sure that you have marked special, inventive language you've seen in your book with Post-it notes? If you haven't noticed any, quickly reread. You may have sped right past those spots! You definitely don't want to miss those."

After a bit, I said, "If you don't think that your book uses language in special ways, then take a break from it and read one of the poems in the basket at the center of your table. One way or another, make sure you find some inventive, playful language to admire and think about. Soon, you and your partner will think together more deeply about one of those examples."

SESSION 6: RECOGNIZING LITERARY LANGUAGE

SHARE

Readers Discuss Literary Language with Their Partner

Remind students of ways they have learned to reread with partners to improve their fluency.

"Readers, do you remember when you learned how to reread with your partner to make your voices smooth?" I pointed to the chart from Bend I and read it out loud to the class.

Add to the partner chart to give students more options of ways to work with partners and reinforce the minilesson.

"When you work with your partner, you can reread for these reasons," I said, as I gestured to the strategies on the chart. "And you can also reread to discuss the literary language you and your partner have found. Work together to clarify its meaning or just to enjoy how it sounds!" Then I added a new strategy Post-it—"Discuss literary language"—to the chart.

ANCHOR CHART

Partners Reread Together to . . .

- Practice out loud and try to picture what's happening.
- Perform! Bring characters to life.
- **Discuss literary language.**

"Today when you work with your partner, you can practice all the ways partners reread," I said as I gestured to the chart. Partnerships began working, and I coached as needed.

40   GRADE 2: BIGGER BOOKS MEAN AMPING UP READING POWER

Session 7

Understanding Comparisons

MINILESSON

CONNECTION

Remind students that many books contain playful, inventive language. Celebrate that your students notice this, highlighting the need for them to figure out what an author is trying to show.

"Readers, you've already heard that those scientists who study reading—the reading professors who go into classrooms like ours with their clipboards (and their pens behind their ears) and watch kids read—have announced that the books you read often contain inventive, playful language."

"Yesterday we saw that was true, not only for *Owl Moon* but also for lots of the books you all are reading. Maddie, for example, was reading *Come On, Rain!* by Karen Hesse, and she said, 'This book has special language on almost every page!' And she's right. Many of you know that book, right? Do you remember how the narrator describes the heat 'wavering off tar patches in the broiling alleyways' and says, 'I am sizzling like a hot potato'?" Then I read aloud the first three pages of *Come On, Rain!*

"As skilled readers of that book, Maddie and the rest of you don't just read, read, read—going through the pages without a pause. Instead, you notice the special ways Karen Hesse uses language, and you think, 'What is it she wants me to see, to feel?' You could say, 'I think Hesse wants readers to know it is a hot day,' but I know you're able to read with even more insight."

IN THIS SESSION, you'll teach children that when authors use comparisons, they are signaling that they want readers to combine their knowledge of both things being compared and how they're alike.

GETTING READY

✓ Prepare to reference a comparison in *Come On, Rain!* by Karen Hesse or any book with illustrative examples of literary language (see Connection and Teaching).

✓ Display the anchor chart "Understanding Literary Language" so it is ready to refer to, and prepare to add the strategy Post-it—"When two things are compared, think about how they're alike." (see Connection).

✓ Prepare examples of literary language in *When Sophie Gets Angry* by Molly Bang or any book where comparisons are made about the characters (see Active Engagement).

✓ Make sure baskets of poetry and books including comparisons, invented words, and figurative language remain on each table for students to use throughout the bend (see Link).

✓ Prepare prompts on index cards to show with the document camera (see Mid-Workshop Teaching).

✓ Prepare an example of literary language in which a comparison of items is used (see Share).

🟢 **Name the teaching point.**

"Today I want to teach you that when an author describes something by suggesting it is like something else—something that actually is quite different—the author expects readers to bring those two distinct things together in ways that create a brand-new, made-for-the-moment meaning."

I added a new strategy Post-it to our anchor chart introduced in the last session.

We referenced Come On, Rain! *in the Connection for examples of comparisons. You can use whatever your students are reading, drawing on examples from your own classroom as you come across literary language in well-written texts.*

> **ANCHOR CHART**
>
> Understanding Literary Language
>
> - Pay attention to special language.
>   1. Notice when words are used in special ways.
>   2. Reread that part.
>   3. Remember what's going on in the story.
>   4. Think, "What special meaning does the author want me to get?"
> - **When two things are compared, think about how they're alike.**

Post-it: When two things are compared, think about how they're alike.

TEACHING

Demonstrate how you note instances of comparative language, asking, "What special meaning does the author want me to get?" and answering by drawing together the two things being compared and considering how they're alike.

"Let's reconsider what Karen Hesse wants us to be thinking. She doesn't just say it's a hot day, but instead she uses a particular kind of special language—she uses *comparative* language. When she talks about the heat wavering off tar patches in *broiling* alleys and has the girl say she is *sizzling like a hot potato*, what is she comparing the hot day to?" I paused to let students think. "And here is my next question: 'What special meaning does the author want us to get?' Remember that answer will come from thinking about the two things she is bringing together to compare and considering how they are alike.

"Hmm, . . . What are the two things? A potato and a summer day? That's odd." I reread. "Wait—I think she is saying the girl is like *a sizzling potato*. And I'm seeing that the comparison is stretched out more, because a few lines away, she says the alley is *broiling*.

You may need to reread a key sentence or two, letting children join you in thinking about the literary language the author uses.

"So what are the things the author is bringing together? The summer day and . . . Could it be cooking? Cooking in the broiler? I'm thinking she's saying that the day was so hot, it was as if they were living in the oven when it is turned to broil. The girl is really hot outside, like a potato in the oven is really hot. What do you think?"

The children agreed. "What an image! Do you know what the oven is like when the broiler is on? If you do, turn and tell people near you what that summer day must have been like." The room erupted into talk.

Debrief in ways that are transferable to another text and another day.

"So I'm hoping you notice that we *could have* just summed up the special language in *Come On, Rain!* by saying, 'It was a *really* hot day.' But we know authors use special language for a reason. They really want us to see or to know something particular. So we ask, 'What special meaning does the author want me to get?' And when the author has compared two things—especially two things that aren't actually all that much alike, like a girl and a potato—we try to understand that special meaning by bringing those two things together and thinking about how they're alike.

"Did you notice that Karen Hesse didn't actually *say* the summer day was like an oven, turned onto broil? She used words that led us, her readers, to create a vivid picture in our minds, helping us imagine what it would feel like to be there. So this is not easy reading work, but it's worth it, because it engages our imaginations and brings the scene to life."

ACTIVE ENGAGEMENT

Channel students to think about a comparison in a book they know well, bringing together the two things being compared, noting the qualities of the things being compared and how they're alike.

"Let's see if we can find a place where the author uses comparative language in this favorite of ours," I said. I used the document camera to show a page from *When Sophie Gets Angry* by Molly Bang and said, "This time, it's your turn to figure out what the author wants readers to get. Work with each other. Go!"

> *Sophie is a volcano, ready to explode. And when Sophie gets angry—really,*
>
> *really angry . . .*

The children talked in pairs and clusters, and I coached, reminding them to think about why the author might be bringing the two things together. "What do you know about volcanoes?" I prompted one child. After he answered, I probed, "So what is the author saying about Sophie?"

After a bit I said, "I'm glad that when you answered the question, 'What does the author want you to see, to feel?' you remembered that when an author has used a comparison, you need to bring what you know about the two things together. Bring not just the facts, but the traits or feelings associated with those two things. So what did you realize when you thought about Sophie?"

This example is simpler than the earlier one, and, of course, that is deliberate, because you are asking kids to do this by themselves.

SESSION 7: UNDERSTANDING COMPARISONS

Dean said, "We said that volcanoes are dangerous. They explode with red-hot lava coming out. So we thought Sophie is dangerous, and when she gets really mad, it's like a volcano."

I nodded, "Is her anger the slow, quiet kind?" and from all around the room came more details. "It's sudden," said someone. "It just erupts—bam!" another added. "She's not angry all that much, but when she is—look out! That's how Sophie and the volcano are alike."

LINK

Remind readers that during reading time, they need to draw on all they have learned about skilled reading, and not just on the focus of today's minilesson.

"Readers, as you head off to your reading spots and your book baggies, will you remember that just because we focused on something new during the minilesson—on literary language, and specifically on comparisons—this doesn't mean that you can forget everything else you know about reading! Right now, look around the charts in this room, and think back in your mind to all the things you have been taught about reading. Make a list across your fingers of a few things you are going to remember to do—things other than notice literary language."

As the children thought, I did so, too, using my fingers to help me list my resolutions.

After a bit, I said, "I hope you are all remembering to log the page on which you start reading, and then at the end of today, the page on which you finish reading. That record will help you know how much reading you're getting done. And if you're starting a new book, recall how important it is to take time to orient yourself to that book, reading the back cover, and looking inside a bit. Are you remembering that as you read, it's important to make sure the book is just right for you? Can you read it smoothly, like you're talking? Are you recalling that it helps to make your voice match the character's while reading with a just-right reading pace?"

Tell children to be alert to instances when authors have used special language, and to mark those places in their books and prepare to talk about them with partners.

"Now add onto that list that, yes, it will be important today to notice when the author does something special with language. Mark those spots, so you can talk about them later with your partner. And, again today, if you just can't seem to find much special language in one of your books, then take some time to read from the basket of poems in the middle of your table."

It is always important to keep prior instruction alive. We have tried to reference prior instruction often in the Links in this book.

CONFERRING AND SMALL-GROUP WORK

Scaffolding Appropriately

IT IS IMPORTANT that you meet with your below-benchmark level students several times each week to support them in a variety of ways. You'll need to continuously monitor their progress, so as you confer, take quick, on-the-spot running records to check in on that progress. Search for patterns in a child's reading behaviors, thinking:

- Does the child pause at unknown words?
- Does the child use multiple strategies to solve unknown words?
- Do the child's miscues fit meaning and syntax? Do the miscues look similar to the actual words?
- Does the child self-correct? At the point of error? At the end of the sentence/line?
- Does the child recognize and define new vocabulary?

Studying students' reading will help you plan next steps. You may notice, for example, that a reader is not attending to endings of words, in which case you can point this out to the child and do some coaching to support that skill. As the student begins to get control of it, your data will show this—and your student's forward progress will be more solid and secure because of your attentiveness.

Use a variety of methods to coach readers in small groups.

As you work with children in small-group cycles, consider also the *kind* of conference or small group that will most help a particular student. It is helpful for you to have a broad repertoire of possible ways to work in small groups with kids, including partnerships, strategy lessons, Reader's Theater groups, shared reading groups, and guided reading groups. The method you choose to use during any small-group lesson will depend on the amount of scaffolding and type of support your students need. For example, if you identify that students need to work on reading with greater expression, a Reader's Theater group may be a great fit!

(continues)

MID-WORKSHOP TEACHING
Using Thought Prompts to Understand Literary Language

"Readers, will you go back to one of the pages where you noted your author using literary language—special language—and in your mind, will you ask that question, 'What special meaning does the author want me to get?'

"If you find yourself coming up with one quick and easy answer, push yourself to see more, to think more. Try using these thought prompts . . ." I displayed the thought prompts on index cards with the document camera.

> *The author could have just written . . . but instead s/he wrote . . .*
>
> *I think the reason s/he wrote it this way is to show . . .*

I left a bit more thinking time, and then I said, "Readers, to really understand that one passage, it can help to think about how it connects with other instances of special language that come before it and after it. Remember how we thought about the sizzling hot potato *and* about the broiling hot alleyway? Recall the strategy you learned during our nonfiction unit of using the whole page to help you think about this bit of special language."

Again, I gave the children time to think. When I thought most of them had gathered some thoughts, I said, "Turn and share what you are thinking." The room erupted into conversation.

After a bit, I channeled students back to their reading, again reminding them to draw on everything they know that good readers do, including being alert to instances when the author has used special language.

SESSION 7: UNDERSTANDING COMPARISONS

Support English language learners in working with figurative language.

As you get your bearings for today's conferring and small-group work, you may want to take stock of which children are reading books in which they're apt to encounter figurative language. You'll find this sort of language is more prevalent in books at levels K and up than in books with less text complexity. If you decide to focus some of your time supporting youngsters who are struggling a bit with literary language, look first to see if you have any English language learners who are reading levels K and above, and bring those children together for some special support.

You may want to start by explaining that this work is hard for any second-grader, but it will be especially hard for English language learners. Consider an idiom like, "It's raining cats and dogs." Even a native speaker hearing the expression for the first time might be confused! With this group, you might collect idioms from familiar books and spend some time figuring out what the expressions mean together. The important thing for children to know is that there is not necessarily a lot of rhyme or reason to these expressions, and therefore, sometimes the work involves simply guessing from context clues.

SHARE

Comparing Creates a Feeling

Highlight the importance of thinking about the feelings associated with specific words, referring to an earlier example from the minilesson and discussing alternative comparisons.

"Readers, will you come to the meeting area? I have something important to talk to you about," I said. Once children had gathered, I said, "Trevor and I got into a conversation today that I want to tell you about. We started talking about how Molly Bang compared Sophie to a volcano. We realized she could have compared Sophie to fireworks, which also explode. But she didn't. Trevor and I wondered why, and when we got to talking about it, we realized that fireworks have a whole different feel than volcanoes.

"What do you think about when you hear the word *fireworks*?" The children called out associations like July 4th, picnics, parades, and music.

"So why *didn't* Molly Bang say 'Sophie is a firework, ready to explode,' and why did she decide, instead, to say she is a volcano? Turn and talk about that." The children talked, saying that volcanoes have a different feel—they are scary and dangerous.

I narrated what the children were saying. "Molly Bang compares Sophie to a volcano and not to fireworks because she is trying to create a scary feeling rather than a fun and festive one. Readers, when you bring two things together, you make connections between the feelings associated with those things."

Engage students in thinking about comparisons that create specific feelings.

I asked the children to close their eyes and imagine sitting near the ocean and hearing the sound of the waves. Then I asked them to think about how they were feeling. I said, "What might you compare the waves to that would emphasize the feeling you have right now? Turn and talk with your partner about how you might finish this comparison: I listened to the waves. They sounded like . . ."

I let students chat briefly. "How about this . . ." I said. "I listened to the waves. They sounded like a toilet flushing." The children laughed. "But they really did!" I said.

"But that doesn't match the feeling," students argued.

"How about this . . ." I said. "I listened to the waves. They sounded like music."

"Yes!" they chimed. "Much better!"

"I was thinking that the waves sounded loud and scary, like thunder," one student said.

"There you go!" I said. "Different comparisons create different feelings. So when you're reading, think carefully about the feeling that the author is trying to create by making the particular comparison she chose to make."

FIG. 7–1   Chart of comparisons

Session 8

Noticing When Authors Play with Words

IN THIS SESSION, you'll teach children that readers notice when authors use language in creative ways, playing around with words. Readers work to understand what the author is *really* saying.

MINILESSON

CONNECTION

Invite students to think about how authors use words in creative ways by sharing some examples and explaining how figurative language works.

"Readers, I was rereading the research bulletin we got a few days ago. Let's read it again."

> Research Bulletin about Second-Grade Readers
>
> Researchers have found that the books second-graders read often contain language that is used in playful and inventive ways. Second-graders who are especially skilled readers pay attention when a writer has used words in special ways because they know that those passages require extra thought.

"Those researchers were right! You've all seen lots of examples of authors using comparative language, right? Yesterday, when I was working with Jeremiah, he was reading *Happy Like Soccer*. He read":

> My shoes have flames and my ball spins
>
> on this spread-out sea of grass with no weeds,

"He said that the shoes didn't *really* have flames—Maribeth Boelts was just trying to show how fast Sierra was running. Have you found other examples of authors playing around with language?"

The children signaled yes, and I gestured to one of them. "Claire was reading *Amelia Bedelia Goes Camping* yesterday!" The room stirred, and I acknowledged that many of the kids knew that book well. "That book is *full* of crazy wordplay, isn't it? Here's one page that Claire read yesterday. Read it to each other and talk about what it means." I displayed a page in which Mr. Rogers is telling Amelia Bedelia, "It's time to hit the road." I read to the class.

GETTING READY

- Print the text of the research bulletin to read to students (see Connection).
- Prepare to read excerpts from *Happy Like Soccer* by Maribeth Boelts, *Amelia Bedelia Goes Camping* by Peggy Parish, or other books with figurative language (see Connection and Share).
- Prepare to read the first few pages of *The King Who Rained* by Fred Gwynne or another book that uses homophones to make jokes (see Teaching).
- Choose a variety of grade-appropriate texts that contain literary language to distribute to each partnership. We suggest including *Happy Like Soccer* by Maribeth Boelts and *Ruthie and the (Not So) Teeny Tiny Lie* by Laura Rankin (see Active Engagement).
- Prepare a reading log, a book, and Post-it notes to model routines. Reading logs are available on the online resources (see Link).
- Display the anchor chart, "Understanding Literary Language" so that it is ready to refer to, and prepare to add the strategy Post-it—"Figure out what playful language really means." (see Link).
- Make sure baskets of poetry and books including comparisons, invented words, and figurative language remain on each table for students to use throughout the bend (see Link).

"Good," said Mr. Rogers

"It's time to hit the road."

"It's time to hit the road?" asked Amelia Bedelia.

"All right."

She picked up a stick.

And Amelia Bedelia hit the road.

The children giggled. Then I let the children talk among themselves about how the author used the phrase, "It's time to hit the road."

Coach students to notice how the author is playing with language by using two meanings for the phrase "hit the road," one literal and one idiomatic.

Name the teaching point.

"Today I want to teach you that sometimes when authors use language in creative ways, readers need to do a bit of extra thinking to understand what is meant. Authors might, for example, play around with words that can mean different things, and sometimes they intend a meaning readers don't expect. When authors do that, readers can stop and think, 'Wait a minute! That's not what it *really* means!' Then they can use what's happening in the story to think about what would make sense."

TEACHING

Cite clear examples of playful language, inviting the children to work to get the meaning.

"Listen to the way this book starts," I said. I read the first three pages of *The King Who Rained* by Fred Gwynne. The first page showed a king, floating in the sky like a rain cloud, with rain falling from him.

Daddy says there was a king who rained for forty years.

After reading, I paused and said, "Hmm, . . . Wait a sec, that's not what it *really* means. The king isn't really *raining*—he's not pouring water onto his people, right? This is definitely a play on language, where the author is making a kind of joke with words. So now I need to figure out what the joke is. Let's see . . . I think the word *raining* is a play on the word *reigning*," I said, writing the words on chart paper for children to see, "which means 'to rule'! So this author is playing with words here. Do you get it?"

It is important to show students how to question the text as you monitor for meaning. Stopping to monitor is essential and enables students to apply their repertoire of strategies.

When the children laughed, I moved on to the next page.

Daddy says there are forks in the road.

The highway in the illustration had table forks paved right into the road. "Readers, are there *forks* like this in roads?"

"No!" the class chimed, giggling.

"You're right—not the kind we *eat* with! When someone says there are forks in the road, they mean that the road splits in different directions, like this . . ." I drew a quick sketch to show a road with several forks. "Another example of wordplay!

"Playing around with words that *sound* the same but mean different things, or that *look* the same *and* mean different things, is just one way that authors play around with language."

ACTIVE ENGAGEMENT

Set students up in groups of four—two partnerships together—to explore literary language in selected texts, in which you have tagged parts that include figurative language.

"I'm going to distribute books that have lots of literary language. Some of it is playful, creative language, and some of it is special in other ways. Will you and your partner sit with another set of partners and work together? You can find the pages I've marked, read them aloud, and help each other get what the author is really saying."

Coach groups as they find, discuss, and analyze the examples of figurative language in the texts.

I distributed books, and started coaching children as they read aloud the examples of playful, special language.

One group read from *Happy Like Soccer* by Maribeth Boelts. A child read this passage:

> Early every game day,
>
> my auntie looks me over good—brushes my hair,
>
> rubs my legs with lotion.
>
> She says, "Have fun and play hard, Sierra."
>
> I smile, but when she hugs me good-bye,
>
> I know she can feel me low around the edges.

The children noticed and talked about the language in the last line, "low around the edges."

I coached one reader, nudging, "What do you think the author meant when she said 'low around the edges'?" I waited as the student thought about it. "Reread that part again," I prompted. "Maybe she meant Sierra is upset," the student answered. "What makes you think that?" I asked. "Saying someone is low sometimes means she's sad," a student replied.

Essentially, you are teaching students to notice homophones and words with multiple meanings. You may decide to continue this work during word study.

Another group worked with a page from *Ruthie and the (Not So) Teeny Tiny Lie* by Laura Rankin. One student read:

> Ruthie's stomach flip-flopped all the rest of the day.
>
> She couldn't remember the answer to 2 + 2.
>
> When Mrs. Olsen read a story, every word flew out
>
> the window.

I listened to that cluster of students and then said to them, "This author couldn't fool you! You figured out that Ruthie's stomach didn't actually flip around. She was just very nervous. And you don't think words actually flew out of the window with wings, right? I love that you are trying to figure out what the author *does* mean when she uses those words in that way. Keep working on that, because I'm dying to know. Remember to say things like 'Could it be . . . ?' or 'I wonder if . . .' Keep wondering!"

LINK

Remind students to fill out their logs, to orient themselves before starting a new book, and to use Post-it notes to mark passages, all through pantomime.

"Second-graders, I'm going to communicate in silence today." I zipped my mouth. Then I held up a reading log, and raised my eyebrows as if to say, "Are you following me? Fill out your log." I then held up a finger to indicate there was more. I showed myself looking over a book, doing a book orientation. Next, I pantomimed reading and inserting Post-its into the text.

Remind students to use their full repertoire of strategies when reading independently.

Then, speaking aloud, I added, "Remember, sometimes authors are playing with language. Make sure you try to figure out what they *really* mean." Then, I gestured to our class anchor chart, read it aloud, and added the new strategy Post-it.

Note that when students are struggling, it's best not to leap in and do all the work for them. Always look for moments of productive struggle, and plan to support and sustain that struggle with probing questions, helpful prompts, strategy reminders, and other scaffolds—or sometimes simply by allowing students time to work through challenges on their own. Students need to do the work themselves to learn how.

CONFERRING AND SMALL-GROUP WORK

Supporting Students through Shared Reading, Guided Reading, and Partnerships

AS YOU PROGRESS THROUGH THE BEND, you may have spotted some students who are struggling to notice and understand literary language. To support students with this work, you might select a text for shared reading that offers multiple opportunities to experience literary language. Songs and poems such as *Chicken Soup with Rice*, written by Maurice Sendak and sung by Carole King, work well for this type of work. As you read with the small group, you can give students pieces of highlighter tape to cover confusing phrases they notice. Then after they read for a bit, you can support the children in rereading and puzzling over the highlighted passages. Remember not to do the work for the kids! Participating in the struggle together is more fun and effective and makes the work enjoyable and accessible.

Start a second round of guided reading with readers who are ready to move up a level.

At the beginning of the unit, you may have led a round of guided reading. Now in Bend II, it may be time to start another round with students who are ready to move up reading levels. Study your running records and your conferring notes, and look to see which students are integrating multiple sources of information and reading with fluency and high levels of comprehension. These students may need more demanding texts to progress in their skill development. After studying the characteristics of the next text level, prepare book introductions that address the upcoming challenges of the next text level and help students successfully face them.

Support the work of partnerships with conferences crafted especially for this important time of the workshop.

Listening to students as they share and read with their partners is essential. As you confer with partners today, consider where you are positioning yourself during the conference. Your goal when conferring with partners is to support the partnership with the work they are doing *together*! It may feel natural to position yourself in front of the partnership or sit next to one partner. Today, try placing yourself behind the partnership as you dip in and dip out. Placing yourself behind the partnership can help you give lean prompts, enabling partnerships to look at each other rather than drawing their attention to you. If you want a partnership to do something, you might prompt a student like this: "Say, 'Show me where the author was making a joke.'" Or like this: "Ask, 'How did you figure it out?'"

MID-WORKSHOP TEACHING
Noticing Literary Language that Is Especially Tricky—Idioms

"Readers, can I have your eyes and ears? There are some types of literary language that you are coming across that are especially tricky! When authors play around with language in creative ways, they might play on the fact that words sometimes have two meanings. But they might, instead, use what are called idioms, which are odd expressions that don't mean exactly what they say.

"For example, have you ever heard someone say, 'No problem! It was a piece of cake!'?" Some kids nodded. "What does it mean?" I asked.

One said, "It was easy."

"Exactly!" I said. "It has nothing to do with cake.

"Have any of you found any idioms in your books?" I paused and then shared a few examples. I said, "George noticed that in his book, it said, 'It was raining cats and dogs.' He knew that it wasn't really raining animals, and the picture helped him solve it. He figured out that meant it was raining really hard."

I scanned the room as I said, "Readers, be on the lookout for these super tricky phrases, and when you find them, use all of your strategies to solve them, including using context clues, like nearby words and pictures. And don't forget to jot some of these phrases down on Post-its to share with your partner."

SESSION 8: NOTICING WHEN AUTHORS PLAY WITH WORDS

SHARE

Literary Language Cueing Intonation

Review the fluency strategy from Bend I of matching your voice to the meaning of the text. Teach students how they can use literary language to help them find the meaning of the text and read it expressively.

"Readers, do you remember in Bend I when you learned to match your voice to the text? You learned to reread and think about what is happening. If it's a scary part of the story, you reread with a scary voice. If it's a happy part, you reread it with a happy voice. Matching your voice to the text is very important.

"Literary language can help you know the tone of voice in which to read a book. For example, in *Happy Like Soccer* by Maribeth Boelts, when she says, 'My shoes have flames,' we know it's an exciting part of the soccer game. Sierra is running really fast, so it needs to be read with an excited tone of voice. In *Amelia Bedelia Goes Camping*, when it says, 'This pound cake got pounded,' you know it's pretty silly for the author to make that joke, so you can use a silly, funny voice for that part.

"Today, when you are reading with your partner, you can practice not only solving the literary language in your books, but also reading the literary language in a tone of voice that matches the meaning." Students began to work together, rereading examples of literary language aloud to each other with meaningful expression.

Session 9

Reading as a Writer—Focusing on Special Language

IN THIS SESSION, you'll teach children that when readers notice special language in a book, they think about the writer's craft and the special meaning the author wants them to get from that language.

MINILESSON

CONNECTION

Engage students in thinking about various ways authors use literary language across books.

"Readers, we are almost done with the part of this unit focused on the special literary language challenges that books can pose, so I have been thinking and thinking about what the one most important thing is that I can teach in this last little bit of time.

"Last night when I was lying in bed, I kept thinking and thinking about possible things I could teach. I thought, 'What are some other fancy-pants ways that the authors of second-grade books use language?'

"And then it was like a lightbulb went off in my mind!"

As an aside, I said, "Did you catch that bit of literary language? Did a lightbulb actually get into my skull? No! You should be thinking, 'How was that moment like a light going off in a dark room?'"

"Anyhow, back to my point. I jumped out of bed and wrote myself a note so I wouldn't forget. And here it is."

❖ **Name the teaching point.**

"Today I want to teach you that you can think about all the strategies you use when you write books and poems, and notice when an author is using them in your books. When you notice what the author is doing, you can try to name it, and think 'What special meaning does the author want me to get?'"

GETTING READY

- ✓ Display charts related to writing craft from writing workshop.
- ✓ Prepare a blank piece of chart paper for jotting down what students say about the literary language they have been learning through writing (see Teaching and Active Engagement).
- ✓ Place Post-it notes at students' reading spots to use for a quick assessment (see Conferring and Small-Group Work).
- ✓ Ask students to bring their writing folders to the meeting area (see Share).
- ✓ Ask students to select a text that they think might contain literary language. They can choose from their baggies or from the baskets of poems and books placed on tables. Help students find literary texts as needed (see Teaching and Active Engagement).

TEACHING AND ACTIVE ENGAGEMENT

Challenge students to name some strategies they have used in writing workshop to create powerful writing and share some of their responses.

"You've learned so many strategies in writing workshop to make your writing powerful. Right now, remind yourself of those strategies. You can look around the room at our writing charts to help. Then share those strategies with your partner." As students turned and talked, many named strategies from our "Poetry Craft" chart, and some referenced an older chart related to narrative writing.

After a minute, I gathered students back to share some of their ideas. "Readers, I heard so many of you remembering all the literary language you have been learning through studying poetry. I heard some kids say that writers can make comparisons and others mentioned using alliteration. I also heard some of you talk about time-passing words and some about repetition." I quickly jotted these down so the students could see them and reference them later.

- Comparisons
- Alliteration
- Time-passing words
- Repetition

Set students up to search their texts for literary language based on what you have taught in writing workshop and what is on your charts.

"To practice this, and to explore a whole bunch of ways that authors do special things with language, search your books for the kinds of literary language you use when you write. Reread part of a book that is filled with literary language, notice and name what the author has done, and then ask that all-important question, 'What special meaning does the author want me to get?' If the author has compared two things, you know to bring those two things together and think about how they're alike. But if the author has done something else—like repeated something, or made time fly, or added a list—talk with each other about why the author might have decided to do that particular special thing."

Coach students not only to find literary language, but also to think about what it means and why the author put it there.

I went over to Maddie, who was rereading *The Leaving Morning* by Angela Johnson. I listened as she read, noticing a theme.

> *We pressed our faces against the hall window and left cold lips on the pane. (p. 2)*

> *We woke up early and had hot cocoa from the deli across the street. I made more lips on the deli window and watched the movers on the leaving morning. (p. 21)*

Revisiting charts from writing workshop can support the teaching in this session. You can invite your students to name qualities of good writing, or refer to an anchor chart you have already used in writing workshop. For example, a chart with strategies for enhancing narrative craft could be a useful resource. An alternative here might be to remind students of a familiar well-written poem or mentor text and ask them to name some strategies they notice the author using.

Students may name different types of literary language based on what you have taught in writing workshop and what is on your charts. Feel free to modify this list accordingly.

So I left lips on the front window of our apartment and said good-bye to our old place, on the leaving morning. (p. 28)

I asked, "What literary language did you see in this text?" She seemed a bit stuck, so I coached her to reread and pointed to the chart listing types of literary language that we'd made earlier.

Maddie noticed that at several points in the book, the kids "pressed their lips against the cold window pane making marks on the glass. Yeah, it repeats!"

"The author is using repetition," I said, "but why? What does Angela Johnson want us to understand?"

"Maybe she repeats that because it is an important action," Maddie suggested. I encouraged her to continue with her good work.

Next, I crouched down next to Dean and listened as he read *Lilly's Purple Plastic Purse* by Kevin Henkes. "What literary language did you find here?" I asked. I prompted him to reread the chart from earlier. "Why did author choose these words?" I asked. He remarked that Kevin Henkes could have said *bag* but chose to use the word *purse*, because when put together with the words *purple* and *plastic*, which start with the same letter, it sounds almost like poetry. I told him he'd found a great example of alliteration, pointing to the word on the chart. "Later today, you might tell your partner why you think Kevin Henkes might have decided to use alliteration in the title." As Dean considered this, I continued to circulate.

I slid over to Emma, who was reading *Happy Like Soccer* by Maribeth Boelts. I listened as she read.

My auntie is asleep, so I tiptoe to the kitchen.

My heart is thumping the way it does when

my teacher calls on me even though I haven't raised my hand.

I dial the first part of Coach Marco's phone number and hang up, shaky.

I prompted Emma to look at the chart from earlier and think about what type of language she was seeing. "Well, the teacher isn't calling on Sierra. The writer is comparing those things."

I probed further. "Why is she comparing Sierra calling her coach to a teacher calling on her when her hand isn't raised?"

"Maybe because they both make Sierra nervous," said Emma.

I made my way over to Carla, who was reading *The Snowy Day* by Ezra Jack Keats. I listened as she read.

As you listen in to coach students, you may notice that they are able to identify the literary language with minimal prompting and support, but you may need to coach them to think about why the author chose to use it.

SESSION 9: READING AS A WRITER—FOCUSING ON SPECIAL LANGUAGE

Before he got into bed he looked in his pocket.

His pocket was empty. The snowball wasn't there.

He felt very sad.

While he slept, he dreamed that the sun had melted all the snow away.

But when he woke up his dream was gone.

The snow was still everywhere.

New snow was falling!

I asked Carla what literary language she'd found. With some prompting, she read, "While he slept, he dreamed . . ." Then, she read the next part, "But when he woke up his dream was gone."

I asked, "What type of literary language is that? Reread the chart from earlier to help you."

Carla suggested that it showed time had passed. "Great," I said. "Sometimes authors use phrases like this to let readers know that time has gone by."

LINK

Share examples of the literary language children have found.

I gathered the class and said, "Readers, you have been finding so much literary language and thinking about what it really means. Each of you noticed new and different ways that authors used literary language. Emma noticed when the author of *Happy Like Soccer* compared two different situations that made Sierra's heart thump. Carla noticed the special way the author talked about the passage of time in *The Snowy Day* with the words, 'But when he woke up his dream was gone.' Dean noticed how the author used alliteration, for example, in *Lilly's Purple Plastic Purse*. Maddie noticed how the author kept repeating a particular phrase over and over again to show that it was important. Some of you also noticed that anytime a character was thinking in the book, the thinking was in italics. As you are reading today and everyday, remember that your books are filled with special literary language, and it's important to think about why the author put it there and how it helps you understand the stories you are reading."

CONFERRING AND SMALL-GROUP WORK

Collecting Data to Assess Quickly

TODAY, like the previous session, you'll presumably divide your time between conferring and small-group work, and you'll probably lead a variety of small groups. You may continue working with the guided reading cycle, and as you think about a second session with the same guided reading group, begin to consider ways to lighten your scaffolding and move students toward reading at this level with more independence. You might give less of a book introduction, or have students coach each other at points of difficulty as they read, while you coach less.

You can continue the shared reading small group you began during the previous session or start one today. If you were doing shared reading of *Chicken Soup with Rice*, you may add more verses to it today. If you prompted students yesterday to notice literary language, try to step back, hand over the highlighter tape, and give students the opportunity to find examples more independently.

MID-WORKSHOP TEACHING
Reading the Whole Page to Figure Out What a Phrase Means

"Readers, can I have your eyes on me for a minute?" I voiced over. "So many of you are finding literary language in your books. It is everywhere! Sometimes, though, it is hard to figure out exactly what the author means. When this happens, you can read the whole page to help you think about what the author is trying to say. Sometimes you can find clues in other sentences before or after the one that seems tricky. And sometimes the picture might provide useful information.

"Don't forget to jot down some of these phrases you are finding on Post-its."

Design small groups to support comprehension.

As you look across your notes and listen to your readers, you may want to convene a couple of small groups to support comprehension. Look to see who may need support in monitoring for meaning across texts. Pull each of these groups for no longer than ten minutes, and have students work first on a shared text and then in their just-right books. Say to readers, "As you read, remember that reading is not just saying words on the page, it is understanding what's going on in the story. Watch me try this." Then, quickly demonstrate reading a bit, and then stopping and saying what has happened so far. After that, you can coach students as they try this in their own books. Say, "Start reading your books, and when I tap you, tell me about what has happened in your book so far." You might then reconvene this group the next day, providing fewer scaffolds.

Quickly assess readers by asking students to place a Post-it with an example of literary language on the corner of their desks.

During your reading workshop, you can collect and analyze data in a variety of ways. One way to quickly take the pulse of the class is by prompting students during independent reading to jot down notes with a specific purpose. Since you are in a bend focused on tackling and using literary language, it's a good idea to monitor students' progress in doing so. You may ask students to jot down on a Post-it a good example of literary language they came across during independent reading today. Then you could quickly scan the results and strategically target which students to confer with or pull into a small group. You might note students who still have a hard time grasping what constitutes literary language. For example, some students may write down a tricky word to decode or a new vocabulary word. In these cases, when you want students to grasp the concept of literary language, you might read with them and practice noticing comparisons and looking for keywords such as *like* or *as*, which can be helpful clues to literary language.

SESSION 9: READING AS A WRITER—FOCUSING ON SPECIAL LANGUAGE

SHARE

Celebrating Literary Language in Reading by Using It in Writing

Explain how reading literary language can help you become a better writer. Remind students of the Post-its they created during the previous session to mark examples of literary language.

"Research shows that good writers are also readers. Reading books with lots of literary language helps us write with lots of literary language. You have been collecting literary language in the books you are reading. Some of you have lots of Post-its noting all the literary language you have found. Today you can *use* all those Post-its!"

Set students up to add literary language that they have been studying to their own writing.

"For partner time today, you'll do something a bit different—you will write! Together with your partner, take out your writing folders, and try to see if you can add some literary language to your writing. You can borrow some of the phrases you have found in your books and jotted down on your Post-its, or you can make up your own. Sometimes the very best writers borrow a phrase or two from other books." Coach students as they use their notes to practice adding literary language to their writing.

FIG. 9–1 Student's collection of literary language

Meeting the Challenges of Longer Books

BEND III

Session 10

Setting Up Routines for Same-Book Partners

IN THIS SESSION, you'll teach children that reading the same books as a partner can help readers talk, clarify, and ask questions to better understand the books they are reading.

GETTING READY

- Ask partnerships to book shop together and select just-right texts with duplicate copies.
- Print the text of the news bulletin to read to students (see Connection).
- Prepare to show a book that students might have been reading in September, a book that they may be ready to read now, and a book they may read in the future. We use *Katie Woo Has the Flu* by Fran Manushkin, *Minnie and Moo Go Dancing* by Denys Cazet, and *Beezus and Ramona* by Beverly Cleary (see Connection and Teaching).
- Prepare to hide a student (e.g., under a blanket or behind an easel), to be unveiled as the "miracle tool" (see Teaching).
- Create a new chart titled "Same-Book Partners . . ." with the strategies listed (see Active Engagement).
- Include duplicate texts in the classroom library to support same-book partnerships (see Link).
- "Questions Partners Ask Each Other" bookmark. A template for this bookmark is available on the online resources (see Conferring and Small-Group Work).
- Make Post-its available for students to use while reading (see Share).

MINILESSON

CONNECTION

Share breaking news from researchers in the form of a bulletin announcing that because the books second-graders read are long, students are at risk of losing the storyline.

"Oh my goodness, you will not believe what I saw in the teaching magazine that arrived in yesterday's mail. Another bulletin from reading scientists about second-graders!"

I displayed the news bulletin for students to see.

> *Breaking News about Second-Grade Readers*
>
> *Researchers report that, because the books second-graders read are much longer than those read by younger readers, second-grade readers face a new risk. As second-grade readers read, there is a clear risk that they can lose the storyline.*

"Second-graders, I read that over and over. So far, the reading scientists have given us good help. Remember they also sent a bulletin suggesting that second-grade books often contain playful, inventive language, which second-graders need to work extra hard to understand. Knowing that helped you be ready for Amelia Bedelia to hit the road and for Sierra's sneakers to be on fire."

Contrast the books children are currently reading with the briefer books they read at the start of the year, and invite them to do some work that will help them hold onto longer stories.

"So when this new bulletin came in, I had to think about it. Could it be true that you guys are reading *much* longer books now than you were at the start of the school year?

"You know what I did? I got out some books that you were reading in September . . . like this one!" I pulled out *Katie Woo Has the Flu* by Fran Manushkin. "And *then* I got out the book I was just about to read to you right now," I said, pulling out *Minnie and Moo Go Dancing* by Denys Cazet. "Those researchers are right about the books getting *much* longer.

"So I figured you'd be willing to do some work to make *sure* you have tools and strategies to hold onto these great big, long stories all the way through the books. You up for that?" The kids all nodded.

❧ **Name the teaching point.**

"Today I want to teach you that when books get longer, it's easy to lose track of the story—sometimes without even realizing it! It helps to have strategies for keeping hold of the w-h-o-l-e story, even when it is getting long and complicated."

TEACHING

Point out that students will soon be reading even longer books, so developing strategies now for holding onto the story is a good idea.

"Have you ever been reading along—la de da, all is well—and then for some reason you lose your place? But when you go to find your place, *all* the pages look unfamiliar to you? You think, 'Did I read *any* of this?' even though you know you did. You realize your eyes were seeing and your mouth was saying the words, but you weren't holding onto the story.

"Readers, before you know it, you will be reading even l-o-n-g-e-r books . . . like *this*." I held up *Beezus and Ramona* by Beverly Cleary. "So you definitely need strategies for holding onto longer stories.

"When a book keeps going and going, it can sometimes be hard to find a stopping place. So, you just keep reading, right? Here is the most important tip I can give you: don't do that! When books are long and complicated, you need to talk and think and write *more*, not less."

Explain that the single most powerful tool for holding onto a storyline is a partner.

"The good news is that I have the most powerful tool in the world to help you hold onto a story—even a long one. Under this blanket is a miraculous tool, one that can make a world of difference to your reading."

By now the children were itching to see what the tool under the blanket was. "Can I have a volunteer to help unveil this miracle tool?" I said. Then, with help from an excited student, I lifted the blanket, and lo and behold, one of the children stepped out and took a bow.

Minnie and Moo are watching th sun go down. Minnie loved it and gave it a 10. Moo was daydreaming and wished for a pair of thumbs.

FIG. 10–1 News Bulletin

You may want to hide your "tool" behind a bookcase or an easel. Building some excitement is the goal.

SESSION 10: SETTING UP ROUTINES FOR SAME-BOOK PARTNERS

"Ladies and gentleman, I present to you the best tool in the world for helping you hold onto the whole storyline in a longer book!" Once children stopped giggling, I spoke earnestly. "Seriously, second-graders, as you read longer books, the most helpful tool available is a partner. So, starting now, you will have same-book partners."

Recruit students to study partnership moves as you model a same-book partnership with a student.

"Will you study how same-book partners help readers hold onto the storyline in longer books?" I asked. "Let's pretend Jeremiah is my partner. Watch as we read the start of our class read-aloud book together—it's a chapter book. Your job is to notice helpful things we do as same-book partners that you and your same-book partner might try, too."

I turned to Jeremiah and said, "What if we read up to the end of chapter one and then stop and remember what we read. Okay?" Jeremiah nodded. "Unless one of us gets confused, and then we can stop anytime," I added. We both began reading—to ourselves, quietly. I displayed the text for the class with the document camera.

A soft wind settled in the trees.

Minnie and Moo sat quietly.

The sky turned pink.

It turned orange and red.

And then the sun was gone.

Minnie clapped.

"Lovely," she said. "Just lovely."

"Ummm?" said Moo.

"That was the best sunset

of the summer.

I'm going to give it a ten!"

said Minnie.

She wrote 10 on her scorecard.

"What did you give it, Moo?"

"What?" Moo said.

"Your score! Tonight's sunset!"

"Sunset?" said Moo.

Minnie sighed.

She put her scorecard down.

Same-book partnerships offer a lot of support, so this could be a good time for children to move into slightly more challenging books. It's also a good time to check that partners are matched according to reading level and productive working relationships. You may want to switch a few partnerships now, in cases where one partner has moved up reading levels past the other partner, or in cases where two children aren't working productively as partners.

It is often helpful to select student partners prior to the minilesson. This will provide an opportunity for partners to rehearse their demonstration.

Same-Book Partners...

- Make plans for stopping to check in after reading a section. *Our Plan: Stop and Talk... Chapter 3, 4, 5*

- Don't just ignore the confusing parts...
  o They ask questions.
  o They reread to figure things out.

- Talk to remember parts of the story together. *At first... But then...*

After a moment of reading I said, "I'm sorry to bother you, but I'm really confused."

"What part are you confused about?" Jeremiah replied. I asked why Minnie scored the sunset.

"Hmm, . . . Good question," Jeremiah said. "Let's read that part together and think about it," he suggested, and we reread the relevant section.

"The sunset was so pretty that Minnie gave it a score, like when a judge gives an ice skater a score in the Olympics. Ten is the highest score!" Jeremiah said enthusiastically.

"Now, it makes so much more sense," I said. "Moo and Minnie are watching the sunset, and it's so pretty that Minnie gives it a high score. Let's read on, and when we get to the end of the chapter, we can stop to remember what we just read."

At the end of the chapter, Jeremiah said, "I got it. In this story, two cows, Minnie and Moo, watch a sunset. It's so pretty that Minnie gives it a ten, but Moo is thinking about something else. Then they see a star, and Moo makes a wish for a pair of thumbs."

"I wonder what Minnie will wish for," I said.

"We'll find out soon," said Jeremiah, looking ahead to the next chapter.

ACTIVE ENGAGEMENT

Suggest that partners share what they noticed you did with your same-book partner. After harvesting their observations, suggest a few key things for partners to do together.

I turned to the class. "I asked you to notice what Jeremiah and I did as same-book partners to help us hold onto the storyline. Will you list what you observed with your partner, and talk about whether you two could do similar work today in your same-book partnership?"

I listened in for a bit, and then I gathered the students back together. "You all have listed some good ideas for same-book partnerships," I said. I lifted my first finger and said, "Partners need to plan for reading a section—maybe a chapter—and then for stopping to talk." Lifting a second finger, I said, "They need to ask questions at confusing parts." I continued to list and name the observations I'd heard. "Partners might need to reread to answer their questions. Partners talk to remember what they just read."

I shared a new partner chart for the bend and added several strategies.

You may decide to add visual support to your chart for this new partner routine. Think of charts like these as how-tos, broken down step-by-step for kids. You might even decide to include picture clues or photographs of your students for each step of the routine.

LINK

Set students up to begin reading the same books as their partners.

"Readers, understanding longer books and keeping track of the storyline is easier when you have a partner by your side. Today, remember to stay linked to each other. Start with the book that you and your partner shopped for in your baggie. After you've read that one, you can choose more from our collection of twin books when it is time for you to book shop." I pointed to the new section of the classroom library.

"Right now, in the meeting area, preview the book together with your partner. You might want to read the first page or two aloud to each other and talk about that part. Then you can plan how much more you will read before you stop to talk again. Put a *stop* Post-it on that page."

"And readers, you *must* stop when you get to the planned stopping spot and wait for your partner to reach it, too. If you reach your goal before your partner does, reread. Once you both get to that spot, talk for a bit, then read more. I won't tell you when to stop and talk."

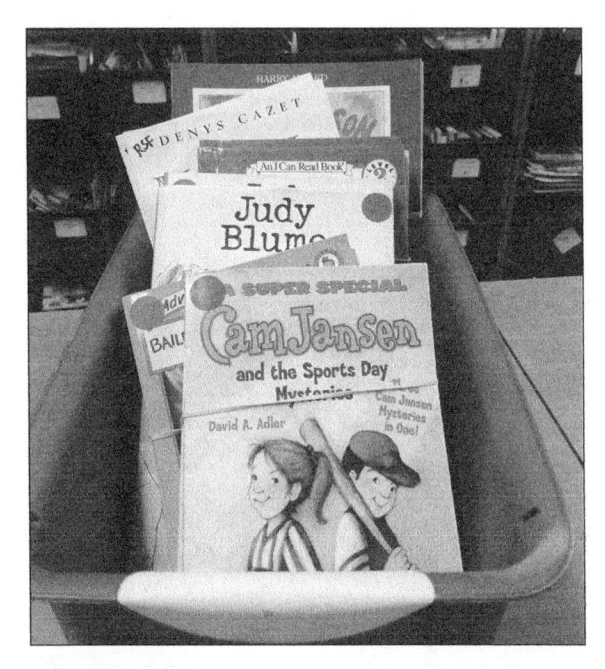

FIG. 10–2   Basket with twin books for same-book partnerships

CONFERRING AND SMALL-GROUP WORK

Supporting Strong Partnership Work for All Readers

TODAY, first and foremost, use your conferring and small-group work time to rally children's excitement about the bend. You've just proclaimed reading partners "miracle tools," and now is the time to make that vision a reality.

As kids read today, you might move from table to table, conducting a little inquiry with each group, posing the question, "How can partners help you understand a book better?" or "What kinds of questions can partners ask each other about stories?" Encourage children to draw on all their past experience as reading partners to name what they can do together to get the most out of their new books. Admire their ideas and add your own. "These are great ideas! I'm thinking that partners can also . . ." Suggest a few strategies for strong partner work.

You might leave behind a tool for partners to use while discussing their books, such as an index card or a bookmark that lists a few questions for them to consider:

- What's happening so far?
- What's this mostly about?
- How is the character changing (or not)?
- What is the character learning? What's the lesson?

MID-WORKSHOP TEACHING Getting Specific

Standing in the middle of the room, I said, "One good thing about being same-book partners is that you don't have to explain what a story is about—your partner knows the details of the story, too! So when you talk about the book, it's okay to get specific! When you talk about confusing parts, make sure you open to those parts in the book and look together at them. Read specific lines, and say things like, "'I think this means . . .'"

Questions Partners Can Ask Each Other

What's happening so far?

What's this mostly about?

How is the character changing (or not)?

What is the character learning? What's the lesson?

SESSION 10: SETTING UP ROUTINES FOR SAME-BOOK PARTNERS

By listing the questions in order of difficulty, you've given them a ladder of thinking to work their way up as they work together. Partners can choose a question to start a conversation or to keep a conversation going.

Support readers who are reading below the second-grade benchmark level, emphasizing retelling, inferring, and determining importance.

Give extra attention to any students who are reading well below benchmark level (i.e., kids who are still reading at levels A–G). It's essential that these children know how to work together as partners in ways that support their comprehension and engagement.

Before they read a new book, partners might look together at the book's cover and the pictures to make predictions about what will happen. Then, as they read, they can pause now and then to check their predictions against what is actually happening in the story. Partners will benefit from reading aloud whole books to each other or taking turns reading pages aloud.

Retelling main events in order, inferring characters' feelings, and determining the main idea of a book are all reasonable expectations of readers at these lower levels, but you may need to offer some basic scaffolding around this work. Suggest that partners take turns retelling parts of the story, building on each other's contributions.

Encourage your struggling readers to talk often about their books. Engagement is essential for children who are reading below benchmark level—books become much more memorable, meaningful, and fun when kids have a chance to talk about them.

SHARE

Readers Become Their Own Partners
Keeping Track of What's Happening in Longer Books

Remind students that this bend is dedicated to supporting second-graders in holding onto the storyline of longer texts.

"Readers, I'm remembering that news bulletin," I said, and then read it aloud again.

"Today, you learned that, to help you hold onto the storyline, it's important to talk, think, and write *more* when you are reading a long book, and I gave you a tool to help you do that. Throughout today's workshop, you and your partner have been talking about the book you are reading."

Point out that, ultimately, readers need to have book conversations in their own minds to track what's happening in longer books.

"But tonight, when you take your book home to continue reading, you can't bring your partner home! So instead, you can read with an imaginary partner in mind, pausing to talk about your book with that imaginary partner in the same way you would with your real partner.

"So right now, will each of you do a silent share? Reread your book, put Post-its on things you notice, things you wonder about, interesting language the author used—and talk those things over silently with your partner in your mind."

After a while, I said, "I can't bear not hearing what you're thinking about, and I'm sure your partner feels the same way. Tell each other what you were saying in your silent share. Go!"

SESSION 10: SETTING UP ROUTINES FOR SAME-BOOK PARTNERS

Session 11

Holding On to Stories Even When Books Are Long

IN THIS SESSION, you'll teach children that, as books become longer and more complex, readers jot down notes on Post-its to keep track of the story and remember the important things that happen.

GETTING READY

- Prepare a book overloaded with Post-its that name itty bitty details, and a book with one very general Post-it at the end, to model examples of unhelpful Post-it use (see Teaching and Active Engagement).
- At the end of each chapter of a book, write a key event on a Post-it to model what might be noted on helpful Post-its. We suggest using *Minnie and Moo Go Dancing* by Denys Cazet (see Teaching and Active Engagement).
- Gather a few items to use to change into character. You may use sunglasses, a hat, a scarf, and so on (see Teaching and Active Engagement).
- Create a new anchor chart titled "Keeping Track of Longer Books" with the first two strategy Post-its—"Ask your same-book partner for help." and "Determine what's important." (see Link).
- Distribute Post-its to partnerships or put them in students' book baggies or at reading spots (see Link).

MINILESSON

CONNECTION

Remind students that when Hansel and Gretel didn't want to get lost in the woods, they left a trail of bread crumbs. Suggest that readers of longer books may need to leave a similar trail to prevent losing the storyline.

"Readers, do you remember that in the story of Hansel and Gretel, when the children are led into the woods by their father, who can no longer feed them, Hansel is smart enough to leave a trail of bread crumbs in the woods so that he and his sister can find their way back home?

"Readers who are working with longer books sometimes need to leave a trail of bread crumbs, too. That way, after they have read a book, after they have traveled the journey of the story, they can go back over the trail they left, remembering each part.

"Only here's the thing. The easiest way to leave a trail as a reader is to use Post-its to mark the path of the story."

❖ Name the teaching point.

"Today I want to teach you that when books become longer, like the ones you are reading now, one way to remember the story is to pause at the end of a chapter to think, 'What's the main event that happened in this chapter?' Sometimes readers leave Post-it notes to remind them."

TEACHING AND ACTIVE ENGAGEMENT

Show a book filled with too many Post-it notes—so many that they provide readers with no help holding onto the main events in a story. Stress that Post-its are most helpful when they note the *most* important things that happen.

"Readers, we talked earlier about how when you read longer stories, sometimes you forget how the part you are reading fits with the rest of the story. It can help to pause at the ends of chapters (or of sections, if there are no chapters), to think, 'Okay, what happened in that part?' You can even jot down a note on a Post-it, so that together, all the Post-its work like a trail of bread crumbs, helping you walk back through the important things that happened across the book.

"I was thinking you could hear from a few readers who tried to do this and think about how well it worked. Sound like a plan?"

The kids were game, so I put on a bizarre hat and sunglasses and said, "Hello, I am Too Too, and I want to show you how I used Post-its to remember the main things that happened in my book, *Minnie and Moo Go Dancing*." Feigning great seriousness, I showed kids a copy of the book that had half a dozen Post-its hanging from *each page*! "I marked this spot on the cow, Moo, because it is shaped like macaroni," I said, "and I put a Post-it on this eyelash because she has one, and . . ."

Taking off the hat and glasses, I said to the class, "What do you think of my friend Too Too and the way he uses Post-its to help him remember the important parts in a story? Turn and talk." The kids cried out that he wasn't choosing important parts and had noted too many small details. I voiced over, saying, "What tips would you give Too Too?" Soon, the kids agreed that Too Too needed to stop and think, "What is the *one* most important thing that has happened in this part that will help me hold onto the story?"

Show a book filled with too few Post-it notes, offering little help in remembering the main events of the story.

Then I put on another wild getup, introduced myself as another character. This time I said, "Hello, I am Onesie, and I want to show you how Post-its help me to remember the main things that happened in my book, *Minnie and Moo Go Dancing*." I showed the kids a copy of the book with only one Post-it at the end.

Then, I said, "I put this Post-it at the end. It says, 'This book is about two cows who want to go to a party at the farmer's house.'"

I took off my disguise and asked the class, "What do you think about the way Onesie used Post-its to hold onto the story in her book?" Of course, the students protested that one Post-it at the very end of the book would not be very helpful because it wouldn't provide enough detail to remember the whole story.

This session will help students stop and jot on a Post-it at the end of each chapter. Some of your students may not have books that have chapters in them. In that case, you can give them some paper clips and coach them to clip a few pages that go together and then stop and jot at the end of their "paper-clip chapters."

Showing children non-examples helps them have a clear understanding of what not *to do, which helps to clarify what they* should *do. Meanwhile, you can have some fun with your students.*

SESSION 11: HOLDING ON TO STORIES EVEN WHEN BOOKS ARE LONG

Demonstrate how to use Post-its effectively to note the main events of the story in a longer book, and help students name why it's especially useful for keeping track of the storyline.

"You game for one more?" I put on yet another silly disguise, this time borrowing a baseball hat from one of my students. "Hi! I'm Professor Post-it," I said. "I'm glad you asked about how I used Post-its with this book, *Minnie and Moo Go Dancing*, because holy moly, those Post-its *really* helped me. See, it is such a long book, and it took me two days to read it, so I really needed my Post-its to track the main things that were happening throughout the story. Here's what I jotted down at the end of the first chapter," I said, as I opened the book to that page.

ch 1: Minnie and Moo watched the sunset, and Moo made a wish on a star for thumbs.

"But I didn't stop there," I said, continuing to play up the character. I read the next two Post-its for the next two chapters, displaying them one by one on the easel like a trail of bread crumbs.

ch 2: Minnie made a wish on a star to go dancing at the farmer's party.

ch 3: Minnie and Moo found old clothes in a trunk and got all dressed up for the party.

FIG. 11–1 Student Post-it at end of chapter

FIG. 11–2 This student told many details and didn't distinguish between the important and unimportant details in the text. If you have students whose retell looks like this, this session will be especially important.

72 Grade 2: Bigger Books Mean Amping Up Reading Power

Invite students to practice reading for the important things, or main events, that happen in their books, and to use Post-its to keep track of those things.

"I'm going to stop Professor Post-it there," I said, taking off the baseball cap and becoming the teacher again, "because now I want all of you to get started reading your shared books. Remember to preview the book, reading the title, back blurb, and chapter headings. Then read the book, pausing at the end of each chapter to think back over what happened and make a Post-it that names the important events."

LINK

Review strategies for keeping track of longer books addressed so far.

"As you read today, remember to ask your same-book partner for help when you need it, and also to use Post-its to note important events in the story as you read." I unveiled the new anchor chart and read the title and first two bullets aloud with some fanfare.

> **ANCHOR CHART**
>
> Keeping Track of Longer Books
> - Ask your same-book partner for help.
> - Determine what's important.
>   - Major events (not itty bitty details)
>   - Problem characters face and how they deal with it

"Get started reading with your partner right now. When I see you and your partner working well, I'll send you back to your seats."

SESSION 11: HOLDING ON TO STORIES EVEN WHEN BOOKS ARE LONG

CONFERRING AND SMALL-GROUP WORK

Supporting Students at All Levels of Text Complexity

STUDENTS READING on or just above benchmark level—those reading early chapter books (levels H–L)—will also benefit from retelling stories as they read, especially to monitor for comprehension. They can stop early and often to retell what's happening so far, and when they aren't sure, that's a sign to go back and reread from the last page where things were still making sense.

> **MID-WORKSHOP TEACHING**
> **Sifting through Post-its, Rereading, and Rethinking**
>
> "Readers, can I stop you for a moment? Earlier I taught you that the most useful Post-its are the ones that help you understand your stories. We talked about how helpful Post-its:
>
> - Name the major event of the chapter.
> - Name the problem that the characters face and how they deal with it.
>
> "But are these the *only* kind of helpful Post-its? What if you want to jot down something that you don't want to forget? Or a really cool literary word to use in writing later? Or a question? Can you use Post-its in those ways, too? Of course you can!
>
> "If you wind up with way too many Post-its like our friend Too Too, it just means you have been doing a lot of great thinking, but you have one last step—a little reading work to do. You can sift through your Post-its from time to time to decide which ones truly are the most important. I like to save the Post-its that I think will help me remember and talk about the story even after I've finished the book. Sometimes it isn't clear which ones will be the most helpful until *after* you've read all of it."

When a student seems to be having difficulty with retelling, often that means that he isn't "wide awake" reading. This student might benefit from working harder to envision the story as he reads, perhaps stopping to sketch on tiny Post-its (the tinier the better to manage the amount of time sketching), or perhaps acting out parts of the story with a partner.

Other students who have difficulty retelling the main events of a story might need to stop and think more often, using a variety of strategies, such as asking questions, making connections, or comparing/contrasting with other stories. These are all strategies you can coach students to practice in conferences or small groups. You might provide these students with a "Stop and Think" sheet listing several key strategies (with picture clues) that they can draw upon each time they stop and think. Then, you can help kids make a clear plan for how often to stop and think; if they are having trouble holding onto key events, chances are they aren't stopping often enough. In an early chapter book, kids who need extra help might purposefully stop and think once per page, once per chapter, once per paragraph, or even after every sentence! In conferences or small groups, you can coach kids to plan appropriately, depending on how challenging the book is. The aim is helping them develop an awareness of reading in an engaged way, rather than passively letting the pages wash over them.

Support students reading longer, higher-level chapter books. Teach them to anticipate the types of challenges their books will present.

While many of your students may be reading at benchmark level, you may also have children in your class who are reading at higher levels—some at M, and perhaps even N or O. It's important that you support these readers, too, so that they can take on the new challenges those levels present. Use your knowledge of book levels to prepare kids for greater text complexity.

Books at level M, such as The Magic Treehouse series by Mary Pope Osborne, tend to revolve around a character, or a pair of characters, facing one big, clear problem that

STOP AND THINK

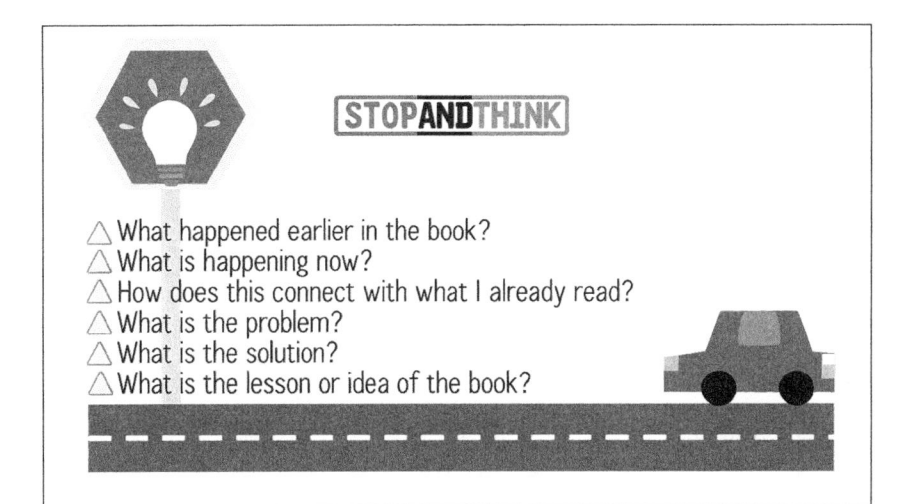

△ What happened earlier in the book?
△ What is happening now?
△ How does this connect with what I already read?
△ What is the problem?
△ What is the solution?
△ What is the lesson or idea of the book?

is resolved by the end. Gather your new level M readers together and explain that they will now have to remember more things that happen and how they're linked, because the chapters in their books will be getting longer. That is, readers at these levels have to do more synthesis work. When something happens toward the end of the book, they might think, "What happened earlier that's connected to this?"

You might point out the importance of previewing books at this level. Tell this group that reading the back of a book and looking at chapter titles can help them anticipate what the story is about so they have that knowledge with them as they begin reading.

If you have readers who are moving toward level N books, let them know that, in these books, the main character often experiences more conflicts. Point out that, although there is still one main problem, there may also be other subproblems. Therefore, in addition to tracking the action across the story, readers will also have to track the problems and their development. Another thing that makes these books more complex is that the characters aren't static—they change from the beginning to the end of the story. Books at this level also include much more figurative language, so readers have to work to figure out what the author is really saying.

Level O books are not significantly different from those at level N, although they tend to be longer. At this level, the secondary characters begin to have more dimension to them, and readers will need to think more about them. Such character complexity becomes even more relevant in levels P and Q books. But it's not just characters—stories at these levels typically don't have just one clear problem, but rather multidimensional problems. The work readers have done earlier is all the more necessary now, and the question, "What seems to be the central problem in this story?" may seem more challenging.

SHARE

Determining Importance Together—Comparing Ideas with a Partner

Ask children to prepare for partner time by rereading Post-its and thinking about their stories.

"Readers, when you and your partner get together today, will you first do a braided retelling of your shared story? That is, one of you starts and retells just a bit of the beginning of the story. Then, the other partner adds a little bit more of the story, weaving in another strand. Then the first partner takes another turn, then the second partner again, and so on, as you continue to add to the story. That way, you'll weave your two memories of one story into a single, coherent retelling.

"After doing that, look back at your Post-its together and think about whether you mostly thought similar things were important to jot down at the end of a chapter. Or did you have very different ideas? Talk about what you notice."

Session 12

Staying on Track When Books Get Tricky

MINILESSON

In the connection, you may tell children, "Readers, earlier I confessed to you that sometimes my eyes are reading and my mouth is reading, but I seem to be in la la land. When I try to remember what the chapter or the book was about, I'm like, 'Huh? What?' A few of you agreed that this has happened to you as well. So I thought this session had better be about how you can take yourself to the reading emergency room when that happens. Because if you are reading and nothing is going on in your head, it is a reading emergency."

A possible teaching point could be, "Today I want to teach you that if you are reading, and you see the text with your eyes but nothing registers in your brain, you need to rush yourself to the reading emergency room and get some treatment started *right away*. The treatment for this problem usually involves slowing down, rereading, and asking questions."

In your teaching, you might say, "I am serious about this. Those researchers who study second-grade readers have pointed out what a problem it is when a reader is reading along, thinking things are hunky dory, when really there is an *emergency*. The story is not getting through to the reader's brain! If the reader doesn't know there's a problem, he might go right through the book, finish it, and say he's done without even realizing he hasn't *read* it at all. He just looked at it!"

To demonstrate, you may want to tell students that the first time you read the seventh chapter of *Minnie and Moo Go Dancing*, you read it without really grasping it. This chapter can be particularly tricky, so it is likely several students may be confused when you finish reading the chapter. You can exaggerate the problem, much as you did with the ineffective use of Post-its.

You may demonstrate by asking yourself some questions at the end of the chapter and then showing yourself being confused. You might say, "Wait, what exactly happened in this chapter? What is going on? I am confused!" Be sure to make this seem like an emergency.

Then you might say, "When this happens, I can use the emergency reading treatment." Remind students of the strategies that can help them in this situation. "I can slow down,

GETTING READY

✓ Display the news bulletin from Session 10 (see Teaching).

✓ Read the first chapter of a demonstration text and display it to the class, perhaps with the document camera. We use *Minnie and Moo Go Dancing* by Denys Cazet (see Teaching).

✓ Display the anchor chart "Keeping Track of Longer Books" and add the strategy Post-it—"When you get off track, stop, reread, and answer questions" (see Link).

✓ Make sure same-book partnerships have duplicate copies of fiction books to read and Post-its to use (see Mid-Workshop Teaching).

reread, and ask questions." Demonstrate rereading the chapter again at a slower pace, making sure you are understanding it as you read by asking and answering questions. Don't read more than the very beginning—just demonstrate how to self-correct. You may point out that when you get to the end of the chapter, you'll ask yourself some questions again, but presumably you won't read enough to actually get there.

In the active engagement, you may ask partners to recap the transferable process that you just demonstrated. You may say, "Readers, think about the steps that I took to fix up my reading. With your partner, name the steps across your fingers. What did I do first, next, and after that to get back on track?" Then, you might listen in to partnerships, coaching students to name the steps in the fix-up process.

In the link, you can add the new strategy to the anchor chart, as you remind students what to do when they get off track. You can let students know that reading emergencies happen, but when they do, there is a cure.

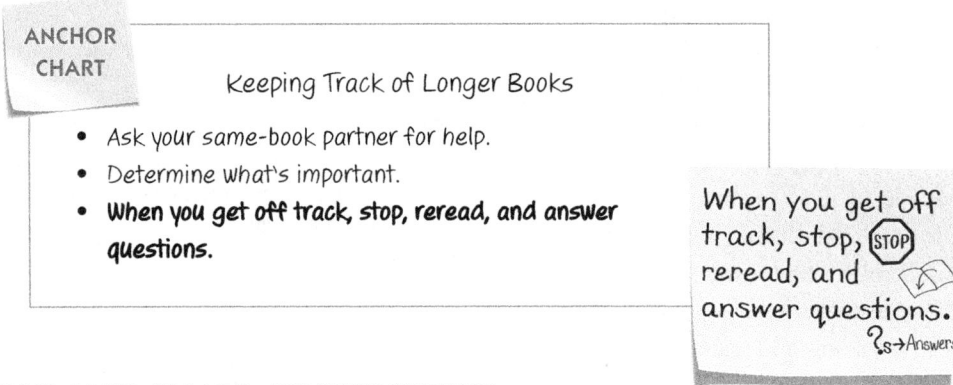

ANCHOR CHART

Keeping Track of Longer Books

- Ask your same-book partner for help.
- Determine what's important.
- **When you get off track, stop, reread, and answer questions.**

When you get off track, stop, [STOP] reread, and answer questions.
?s→Answers

CONFERRING AND SMALL-GROUP WORK

As you confer with individual children and pull together small groups, you may have noticed that a handful of readers tend to read with blinders on. They see the page they are reading, but they don't think about how that page connects back to earlier pages. Gather these readers together for a strategy group on this very skill—connecting later parts of a story to earlier parts. Tell them why you've gathered them, and then introduce a demonstration text to show them how to connect parts of a story together.

You might show students a book in which the main character clearly changes from the beginning to the end, such as *Poppleton and Friends* by Cynthia Rylant. Read aloud the part at the beginning in which Poppleton thinks going to the movies alone is a great idea because he can eat all the popcorn by himself and won't have to listen to anyone else talking. As you read a bit more, point out to students that Poppleton is probably thinking, "This is great! I am getting just what I wanted—to go to the movies by myself." Name how this connects to the earlier part where he said he wanted to go the movies by himself, and then read on.

You can then read through the part where Poppleton has no one to laugh with or cry with, and eating all the popcorn makes him sick. Say something like, "Hmm, . . . maybe Poppleton is thinking that he really doesn't like going to the movies alone after all." Coach kids to think back to the beginning and middle parts, and to notice how all the parts together show that Poppleton has changed or learned something. You might coach them to say, "In the beginning, Poppleton . . . in the middle . . . and at the end . . ." Children should realize that at the beginning, Poppleton wanted to go to the movies by himself, in the middle, he gave this a go, and in the end, he didn't really enjoy it.

This may sound like it isn't a big deal—of course kids would connect the beginning of the book to the middle and then to the ending—but lots of readers of J/K books tend to read with blinders on. They see the page they are reading, but they don't think about how that part connects back to earlier parts of the story. In a small group, you can tell your readers about this observation, and let them know that you have gone through the book they are just about to read and marked some "look-back" pages. You can suggest that they read the book in partners (either silently or aloud to each other), and when they come to a look-back page, they can stop and talk about how that page links back to earlier pages. Scaffold this for a bit, pointing out places where readers might connect to prior pages. Then you can remove the scaffold and suggest that readers determine those pages for themselves—and for each other, too.

As students continue this work, you can let them know that there are predictable ways in which parts link together. One is that something happens, and an earlier part can explain why that thing happened. Another is that something happens that relates to a problem set in motion earlier. Or, in the case of Poppleton, the character changes his mind about something mentioned in an earlier part of the text. Remember that these students are just moving on from books where each chapter was its own little story, so showing how chapters build on each other can facilitate their understanding of the text.

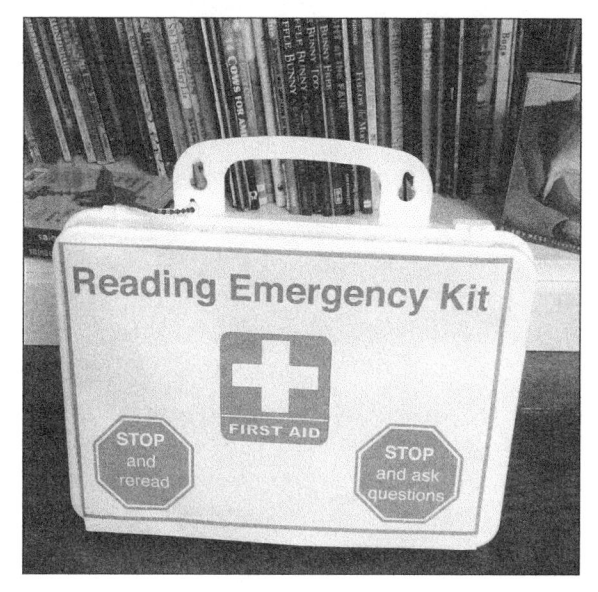

FIG. 12–1 Making reading emergency tool kits filled with Post-its and strategies can engage students.

Mid-Workshop Teaching

In your mid-workshop teaching, stop students to let them know that they could be having a reading emergency and not even know it. Sometimes reading emergencies go unnoticed until it is too late. One way to know if you are in the middle of a reading emergency is to make sure you can make a Post-it at the end of a chapter or every few pages. If you don't know what to write on the Post-it, that's a sign that there is a reading emergency happening. You can then remind students of what to do in a reading emergency by reviewing the anchor chart.

SHARE

In your share, you may want to remind students of their same-book partnership routines, referencing the chart from Session 10. Suggest that when readers get together with a partner, that's a good time to say, "Help!" or "I tried this, but I still have some trouble understanding this part." Give students some tips to help their partners, such as rereading the tricky part, slowing down, and talking about the part together.

Session 13

Using Writing to Solve Reading Problems

IN THIS SESSION, you'll teach children that readers can invent ways to use writing to help them tackle confusing parts in their reading.

GETTING READY

- Prepare "reading emergency kit"—a pencil and a small stack of Post-its—one kit for each student, plus one kit for demonstration (see Connection, Teaching, and Active Engagement).
- Choose a familiar read-aloud text for demonstration and practice of using writing to keep track of stories. Project the text to the class, perhaps using a document camera. We use *Minnie and Moo Go Dancing* (see Teaching and Active Engagement).
- Prepare chart paper to note common reading problems with longer books (see Teaching).
- Display the anchor chart "Keeping Track of Longer Books" so that it is ready to refer to and prepare to add the strategy Post-it—"Write notes to help you keep track." (see Link).

MINILESSON

CONNECTION

Tell children that there are emergency kits for different problems in the world, and suggest what kinds of troubles a reading emergency kit might help readers tackle.

"Readers, yesterday we talked about how sometimes, with the loooooong stories you are reading now, you get into reading emergencies. The story stops making sense.

"Did you know there are emergency kits to help in different types of emergencies? When I was a kid, my parents always had an emergency kit in our car for times when the car broke down. In it, there were jumper cables to start the car in the case of a dead battery. And there were pink cones to put out on the road, around the broken-down car, so other cars wouldn't crash into it. And there was—this is true—a tinfoil blanket, which was supposed to keep us warm if we had to wait for help in the cold. There were also first aid emergency kits with various medical supplies.

"I've been thinking that maybe we should make reading emergency kits, so whenever you run into trouble as a reader, you'll have tools to help you out. To help me design that kit, I started listing trouble you sometimes get into.

1. I know that it's easy to mix up characters, like Frog and Toad ('Which is the one who sleeps all day?'). So I thought, 'One common problem is mixing up characters.'

2. Sometimes, as we discussed yesterday, you worry so much about reading the words that you push through with your mind turned off, so when you get to the end of the book, *you can't even remember it!* You go to retell it, and you go, 'Huh? Ahhhhh . . .'

3. Sometimes you think you're remembering the story, but all these things are happening and you don't know why they happen or how they fit together. That's a clue that you aren't following the story.

"And I am sure there are other kinds of trouble you run into as a reader. So having an emergency kit to help you handle your reading troubles could be really helpful!"

❖ **Name the teaching point.**

"Today I want to teach you that, as a reader, you can have your own reading emergency kit ready, as long as you have this . . ." and I held up a pencil. "If you know how stories get confusing, you can invent ways to use writing to help you sort out those confusing parts and keep track of the story."

TEACHING

Suggest that readers figure out writing tricks to help them tackle reading troubles. Share one—a labeled pencil sketch—to help you differentiate two characters.

"Readers, maybe for you, reading was once all about saying the words, one after another. But as stories get longer and the thinking part of reading becomes a bigger deal, I think you are realizing that reading is also about inventing and using strategies that can help you when you find yourself in a reading emergency situation. To solve the emergency, readers figure out little tricks to help with whatever problems they encounter trying to keep track of the characters and events in a story and how they are connected. And many of those tricks involve using a pencil.

"For example, is there any reader in this room who has read a Frog and Toad book and not been clear which character is Frog and which is Toad?" Some kids sheepishly poked a little hand up. I joined them, with much more enthusiasm. My hand shot up. "I definitely have that problem! I keep thinking, 'Which one is which?'

"But the good news is that when I have a problem like that—confusing Frog and Toad—I have my handy dandy little reading emergency kit," and I pulled out a pencil and two Post-its. "Watch," I said, and then I drew Frog and labeled him "green," and Toad, and labeled him "brown." "I keep these pictures near me as I read. I even add to them as I read, so after a bit they look like this." I put words on each Post-it describing the character's personality.

Debrief. Explicitly name what strategy you just modeled for students. In this instance, you sketched and labeled characters.

"Did you see how I just used a little bit of writing to help me fix my reading emergency? I sketched each character, and then I labeled each one with some identifying information, so that I could keep them straight while I read.

"But mixing up characters isn't the only reading emergency that ever happens, is it?" I recalled the common problems we'd discussed, and listed them on a chart for reference.

You may notice your students facing a variety of challenges as they learn to keep track of their stories, and you can of course revise your "trouble list" based on your students' specific needs.

SESSION 13: USING WRITING TO SOLVE READING PROBLEMS

Common Reading Problems with Longer Books
- Mixing up characters
- Forgetting what happened
- Wondering how things fit together

Model a second way to use writing to solve problems while reading—jotting down the important things that happen.

"Another common problem is having a hard time remembering what happened. So let me take my reading emergency kit and think about what can I write to help me solve this problem." I paused to think for a moment. "Oh, I know! Maybe as I read, I can write down all the big things that happen in order.

"Watch as I read a bit of chapter two in *Minnie and Moo Go Dancing* and write down what is happening in order."

Chapter 2: The Second Wish

"Thumbs?" Minnie said.

Moo nodded.

"Yes," she said, "Thumbs."

She looked at the farmer's house.

Bright light lit up the night.

People laughed.

They danced to music.

"We are only cows," said Moo sadly.

"Without thumbs . . .

we will never dance."

Minnie put her arm around Moo.

"Moo," she said.

"You don't need thumbs to dance.

It is true people have thumbs.

With thumbs,

people can make things.

But . . . can they make happiness?

Your class may name different challenges they have encountered while trying to understand their stories. It doesn't matter which problems they identify, as long as they name some. Then you can teach them how to address those challenges using writing.

It is important to emphasize that students can use any type of writing to solve their problems. They do not have to create a timeline or a web or anything in particular. This strategy is about students using writing in inventive ways to help them meet reading challenges.

> *Moo thought about it.*
>
> *"We have friends," Minnie said.*
>
> *"We have a warm barn in winter.*
>
> *We sleep under the stars*
>
> *in the summer.*
>
> *And we get milked every day!"*
>
> *". . . with thumbs," added Moo.*

"Okay, let me think what just happened." I picked up a pencil and wrote on a Post-it, "Moo wants thumbs. Minnie tells Moo they can still be happy without thumbs." I said, "Readers, did you see how I read a bit and then wrote down the important thing that happened? Let me keep going." I read the next part of the chapter.

> *Minnie and Moo sat quietly.*
>
> *A second star appeared.*
>
> *"I just made my wish," said Minnie.*
>
> *"Come on, Moo. Let's go!"*
>
> *"Where are we going?"*
>
> *"Dancing!" said Minnie.*

"Now let me write down what just happened." I picked up my reading emergency kit again, and took out another Post-it. "A second star appears, and Minnie makes a wish to go dancing." I turned to the students. "Wow, readers, do you see how I am writing down the big things that are happening? I understand what is happening so much better! This time, I used writing to help fix the problem of keeping track of events."

ACTIVE ENGAGEMENT

Invite students to try out the strategy of using writing to solve common reading challenges.

"Readers, now it's your turn to try. Many of you said that figuring out how things fit together can be tricky, especially when there are a lot of different things happening. So, I thought we could practice this together, inventing a way to keep track of them. There isn't a right or wrong way to do this," I said.

I held up *Minnie and Moo Go Dancing* again and showed it to the children. I said, "I know some of us are wondering how all that is happening in the story fits together. So I thought you could invent ways to use writing to keep track." Then I read from the next chapter.

It is important to encourage students to create their own graphic organizers and reading notes. This is higher-level work than having students fill in a graphic organizer you created.

Minnie opened an old trunk.

She pulled out a purple prom dress.

She held it up to Moo.

"It's you!" said Minnie.

"It's beautiful," said Moo. "But . . ."

Minnie smiled.

"We're going to a party," she said,

"and we don't need thumbs!"

"Hurry," said Moo.

"I know how all of this goes on.

I saw it in a magazine once!"

Minnie and Moo squeezed

into their dresses.

"This girdle thing

goes on the outside," said Moo.

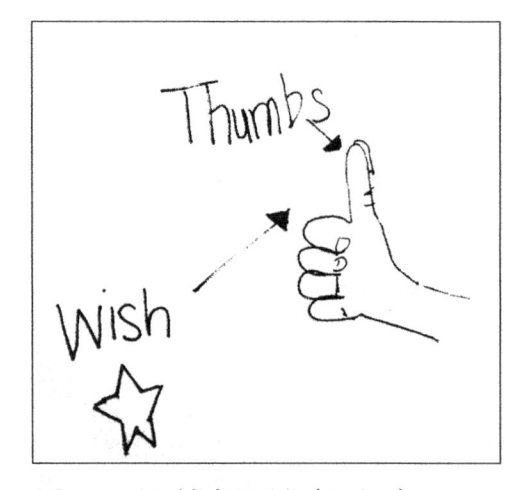

FIG. 13–1   Maddie's Post-it showing how Minnie wished for thumbs

FIG. 13–2   Carla's Post-it showing Moo squeezing into a party dress

"Right now, use your reading emergency kit to invent a way to help you think about how things fit together." I gave students one minute to work on their tools and notes.

Display tools students created and notes they wrote. Name what they are doing to help themselves keep track of what's happening in the story and how things fit together.

After a moment, I selected a few Post-its to display with the document camera. I picked up Maddie's Post-its and showed them to the class. "Look! Maddie jotted down 'thumbs' and then 'wish,' and she drew a star. Maddie was wondering why Minnie brought up 'we don't need thumbs.' Then she remembered it was the wish on a star, so she wrote it down next to the word 'thumbs,' because that is how those things fit together. Great tool, Maddie!" Then I showed Carla's Post-its with the document camera. "Look, Carla has drawn a little picture of Moo squeezing into her dress, and then she wrote 'party' at the top. Carla is connecting that Moo is putting on the dress and girdle so she can go to the farmer's party. Great connection, Carla!"

LINK

"Readers, you can take these toolkits with you to your reading spots today. Remember, you can always use a little bit of writing to help you solve reading emergencies. Name what is hard for you about reading longer books, and then think about how you can use writing to help." I added this strategy to the anchor chart.

ANCHOR CHART

Keeping Track of Longer Books

- Ask your same-book partner for help.
- Determine what's important.
- When you get off track, stop, reread, and answer questions.
- **Write notes to help you keep track.**

SESSION 13: USING WRITING TO SOLVE READING PROBLEMS

CONFERRING AND SMALL-GROUP WORK

Priming the Pump for the Final Bend

AT THE END OF THIS BEND, it's a good idea to gather together students who are still struggling with understanding their stories and review all the work of the bend with them. You may choose to practice with a shared text. As you read the text together, periodically ask students to stop and name what has just happened in the story. Teach kids to use retelling as a tool to help with monitoring for meaning. Have students retell the story from the beginning each time you stop to practice building a cumulative understanding of the text.

When retelling starts to break down, that's a sign to reread from the last place where things were still making sense—and to reread differently. You might coach students to pay more attention to how characters feel, not just what they are doing. Or you might remind students to pause more often to picture the story in their minds—and to imagine that picture in motion—more like a movie than a photograph. Some students may need some coaching to use more expression in their voices as they read to bring the story to life. In any case, the retelling might not improve simply by practicing more retelling—it's the work students do *as they read* that will ultimately lead to a stronger understanding.

As you continue, you might pass off responsibility to partners to help each other stop and retell what has happened so far, coaching as needed. Some students may have trouble determining importance—they may find things important that aren't, or they might miss important details. Over time, plan to teach these students a few strategies for determining importance. To figure out whether something is important, for example, they might ask themselves if it's connected to the main problem in the story, or they might notice if it's linked to a big feeling.

One problem you may notice is students not realizing they are not comprehending. These students keep reading and don't know that they need to stop and use fix-up strategies. When this happens, remind them that readers monitor their understanding

> MID-WORKSHOP TEACHING
> **Sharing Tools and Notes Students Generated**
>
> "Readers, can I stop you for a second? You have created some great tools." I showed Philip's Post-it with the document camera. "Look! Philip wrote some notes to help him think about Poppleton. He wrote 'Poppleton' in the middle of the Post-it, and then he noted things he learned about Poppleton to help him keep track of what he knew about the character."
>
> I displayed Dean's notes next. "Dean has three Post-its to keep track of his characters Pinky and Rex. He put things about *just* Pinky on one Post-it, and things about *just* Rex on another, and everything that overlapped between the two characters on a third Post-it. For example, they have the same number of stuffed pets." I gave students a moment to take in the different kinds of notes students had made.
>
> "On the table at your seat, place whatever you wrote to help you keep track of your story. Then, take a quick look at what others at your table created. Maybe you'll be inspired to try something you see!"

as they read. You might gather these students in a group. You can put little stop signs on Post-its at various points in a book at their level—perhaps at the end of a chapter or when something big happens. Tell students that when they see one of these stop signs, they should stop and ask themselves some questions, such as "What has happened so far?" and "What is going on with the characters right now?" Coach students as they do this work. As you continue to work with these students, you can put fewer and fewer stop signs in their books as monitoring for meaning becomes more automatic.

Gather some data to support the upcoming work in Bend IV.

Soon, students will be selecting reading goals to guide the formation of goal clubs. It is important to have a sense of what students are struggling with in this unit, so you can guide them toward a club that will support them in an area of need. This may be a good day to conduct some more dip-in and dip-out conferences. In these conferences, you can listen as students read for how they are doing with fluency. You can ask them about literary language, and you can ask them to retell the story. You may find that some students are stronger or weaker in one of these areas. Jot this information down, so when it comes time to choose a club, you can steer them in the right direction. Then offer a tip or two before you leave.

SHARE

Celebrating Understanding Longer Books

"Readers, you have been working so hard to understand the longer books you are reading. You have a lot to keep track of, but with the help of your partner and your reading emergency kits, you can do it! Today when you meet with your same-book partner, you can celebrate understanding your longer books. When you understand a book really well, you can do one of these things:

- Act it out together.
- Tell it as a story.
- Discuss the big lessons.

"When you meet with your partner today, choose one of those things to do to celebrate all you have done to understand your book."

Tackling Goals in the Company of Others   BEND IV

Session 14

Self-Assessing and Setting Goals

IN THIS SESSION, you'll teach children to self-assess their own reading in order to set goals. They will work with a reading club to help each other reach those goals.

GETTING READY

- Display anchor charts from each bend together—"Making Your Reading More Fluent," "Understanding Literary Language," and "Keeping Track of Longer Books" (see Teaching).
- Choose a shared text for demonstration and practice. We use an excerpt from *Happy Like Soccer*. Display the text, perhaps using the document camera. Prepare Post-its to label the strategies you model. Distribute copies, highlighters, Post-its, and pens to students (see Teaching and Active Engagement).
- Distribute Post-its in students' reading baggies to use to write their name and their reading goals (see Mid-Workshop Teaching).
- Distribute copies of anchor charts and tip sheets to each goal club: Fluency Club, Literary Language Club, and Keeping Track of Longer Books Club (see Share).

MINILESSON

CONNECTION

Ask children if they have ever been part of a club, and talk up the benefits of reading clubs.

"Readers, it has been so amazing to see you working with your partners, helping each other understand your books better. If it's so great to have one partner, imagine how great it would be to have three or four partners!" Students' eyes grew big.

"Have any of you ever been in a club? A Lego club? A science club? A gymnastics club? Well, we can have clubs in our reading workshop, too! Clubs help us stay focused on a shared interest and get better at it together. We can join clubs to become stronger and stronger in our reading."

❖ **Name the teaching point.**

"Today, I want to teach you that readers stop and think about their reading work, asking, 'Do I need more work with fluency? Understanding literary language? Tracking the stories I read?' Then, they set goals and work with others to make a plan to reach those goals."

TEACHING

Display anchor charts from each bend at the front of the room to review all the work of the unit.

I pointed to the anchor charts from each bend of the unit that I had hung at the front of the room. "Look at all we have learned in this unit! We've learned about *three* really major things over the past few weeks." I pointed to each chart as I named the major work of each bend. "One thing we have learned is to make our voices smooth and expressive." I pointed to the anchor chart from the fluency bend. "A second thing we have learned is to pay attention to special language." I pointed to the literary language chart. "And a third thing we have learned is to keep track of what is happening in longer books." I pointed to our latest anchor chart.

"Today I want you to think about which of these strategies you feel really strong using on your own, anytime you are reading, and which of these strategies you might want to spend more time practicing."

I gave students a moment to review the charts and begin reflecting on their own reading progress.

Invite students to use the charts as tools for self-assessment and goal-setting.

"Later today, you'll have a chance to choose which chart, of all these charts, is the one that would help you the most as a reader right now. You'll be choosing the one with strategies you need to practice the most to help you work toward a reading goal you want to meet. Then, I'll set you up with other kids who chose the same chart, so that you can work together toward your goal—you'll be a reading club!"

As I displayed the first page from *Happy Like Soccer* with the document camera, I said, "Watch how I use the charts to help me stop and think about my reading work, asking, 'Do I need more work with fluency? Understanding literary language? Tracking the stories I read?' Then, I'll pick one of these charts to help me work toward my goal."

Model reading and annotating the text, noticing literary language.

"I think it's helpful to think about one chart at a time and sort of test myself to see if I'm really doing everything on the chart. Let's start with 'Understanding Literary Language.'" I pointed to the chart, and then I began to read the page.

> NOTHING MAKES ME HAPPY LIKE SOCCER—
>
> picked for this new team,
>
> with these shiny girls.

I read the first sentence out loud and paused. "I see some literary language," I said. "Thumbs up if you see it, too!" I paused and allowed a few seconds of wait time as kids reread the first few lines. As more thumbs went up, I highlighted "shiny girls."

As you launch this bend, keep in mind that having students select their goal clubs supports their capacity to self-assess their own reading and to become more independent.

You may need to support some readers in selecting a goal club. Ask questions to help students discover where they need additional practice.

ANCHOR CHART

Understanding Literary Language

- Pay attention to special language.
   1. Notice when words are used in special ways.
   2. Reread that part.
   3. Remember what's going on in the story.
   4. Think, "What special meaning does the author want me to get?"
- When two things are compared, think about how they're alike.
- Figure out what playful language really means.

I continued thinking aloud. "I know the girls aren't *actually* shiny. Maribeth Boelts is using literary language. So I can think, 'What special meaning does the author want me to get?'" I pointed to that bullet on the "Understanding Literary Language" chart. "Hmm, . . . Think along with me. What does she *really* mean here? Thumbs up when you have an idea."

As kids thought and thumbs started to go up, I placed a Post-it right next to the phrase to label the strategy. "What special meaning does the author want me to get?" I said. "I think Maribeth Boelts means that these are new friends for Sierra, and she used the word *shiny* to mean very new.

"Did you see how I used the chart to help me practice some reading work, to check myself, to see if I can do it? What do you think? Should I pick this one as a goal to work on?" I paused, and kids shrugged. Some said yes, and some said no. "Maybe? Maybe not? Okay, let me keep going. I should probably try all the charts before I settle on one."

Model reading and annotating strategies to make reading more fluent.

I turned to the "Making Your Reading More Fluent" chart and said, "Now let me try using this chart, to see if fluency is something that I might choose as a goal to work on." I read the next sentence out loud, reading in a very choppy, word-by-word fashion.

> My shoes have flames and my ball spins
>
> on this spread-out sea of grass with no weeds,
>
> fields with no holes, and real goals,
>
> not two garbage cans shoved together
>
> like in the lot by my apartment,
>
> where soccer means
>
> any kid who shows up can play.

Again, I reflected aloud. "Whoa! That was a long sentence. Readers, what do you think? Thumbs up if you think my reading was just fine." No thumbs went up. "Thumbs up if *maybe* this could be a goal for me to work on." This time most kids gave me a thumbs up.

"Okay, readers, you're right. My voice didn't sound very smooth. Hmm, . . . What can I do to make it smoother? Let me check the chart." I pointed to the bullet on the fluency chart that read, "Scoop words into longer phrases," and said, "Now I'll reread it, and I'll use the commas to help me know which words to scoop into phrases." As I reread the sentence more fluently, I used the highlighter to show phrasing, highlighting each line up to the comma. Then I labeled the strategy with a Post-it: "Scoop words into phrases."

You might notice how we use thumbs up as a way for students to participate along with the teacher. This increases engagement and active listening, while keeping up the pace of the lesson.

ANCHOR CHART

Making Your
Reading
More Fluent

- Reread aloud and in your head.
- Scoop words into longer phrases.
- Talk like the characters.
- Make your voice match the mood.
- Read with a just-right pace.

Model reading and annotating strategies to keep track of longer stories.

"Alright, now I know fluency might be my goal as a reader, but let me check to see how I'm doing with keeping track of what's happening in the story. Maybe I need even *more* practice with this chart." I gestured to the "Keeping Track of Longer Books" chart.

"Hmm, . . . Let's see if I can reread this page and determine what is important," I said as I pointed to the bullet on the chart. Then I reread the page. "Hmm, . . . Think with me, readers. What's really important here? When you have an idea, give me a thumbs up." I paused just a few seconds as students thought along with me. "I'm thinking that what is really important here is that Sierra is on a new soccer team. It seems like this team is really serious about the game." I made a bracket around the chunk of text and noted the strategy with a Post-it: "Reread to determine what's important."

Recap the process of self-assessment and goal-setting you just modeled.

"Readers, I just tested myself using each of the big charts from our unit. I checked myself to see if I was noticing literary language." I pointed to the "Understanding Literary Language" chart. "I tried reading fluently." I pointed to the "Making Your Reading More Fluent" chart. "And I checked to see if I was keeping track of the story using the 'Keeping Track of Longer Books' chart. Did you notice how with each chart, I tried out one of the strategies, and I noted them so that I could really see the work I was doing as a reader? Whisper to your partner—what do you think I should choose as my reading goal?"

ACTIVE ENGAGEMENT

Distribute a copy of the shared text and a highlighter to annotate parts of the text.

"You'll each get a copy of part of our shared reading text to highlight." I passed out photocopies of page 2 of *Happy Like Soccer*. "You can read this page and practice using the charts in our room to help you reflect on your reading and decide which skills you think could use more practice. Try doing what I did—practice the work from one chart at a time. Mark up parts that you can use to practice getting better at figuring out what special language means, changing your reading voice, or rereading to fix up, smooth out, or think more about the text." I walked around and coached students as they did this, stopping periodically to voice over tips like, "Use the charts to remember the strategies," and "Don't forget to jot down the strategies you're using."

Invite students to consider possible reading goals.

"Now, think about the work you just did. There are three big skill sets we have focused on during this part of the unit: understanding literary language, reading fluently, and keeping track of what's happening in stories." I gestured to each chart as I said this. "So right now, think about this: when you just read that part of *Happy Like Soccer*, which of those skill sets seemed really easy, and which took a bit more work? Turn and talk to your partner." I listened in as students talked.

ANCHOR CHART

Keeping Track of Longer Books

- Ask your same-book partner for help.
- Determine what's important.
- When you get off track, stop, reread, and answer questions.
- Write notes to help you keep track.

Modeling just one strategy from each of the three anchor charts from the unit can help set students up to think about which of the big skill areas they might choose for their goal clubs.

Students may or may not highlight or annotate the text in the manner that you demonstrated. Keep in mind that the important thing here is that they are practicing assessing their own reading. Highlighting and annotating can make this activity more visible and engaging, but they are not essential.

"You'll choose your goal club at the end of reading workshop today, and when you do, be honest with yourself. Which of these is the best goal for you right now? Which skills could use more practice? If one of these skill areas is harder for you than the others, pick that club, so you can get better at those skills."

LINK

Set students up to be reflective readers during independent reading time.

"Later today, you'll decide what club to join. But before that, you'll have time to read independently. As you read today, use all three charts to help you. Think about what you would like to focus on during the final bend in our unit. It's a big decision to make. You'll spend the next few days working with this club to develop that one skill set, so choose wisely."

One of the goals of this bend is to help students manage their own learning. Resist the urge to assign goal clubs based on your assessments; instead, try to help students navigate toward the goals that best meet their needs.

CONFERRING AND SMALL-GROUP WORK

Helping Students Self-Assess to Launch Clubs Smoothly

Coach students to choose a club.

During reading workshop today, you'll probably want to help students choose goals wisely. The challenge will be to help students self-assess rather than assigning them goals. You could start these conferences by asking what is easy for students and what is hard for them as readers. You may follow up by asking them for specific examples of times reading has been easy or times reading has been hard during this unit. You could then guide students to choose goals that will help them work through those times reading has been hard.

Some students may feel that a certain goal is for them—but you may feel another goal is more appropriate, according to your observations and assessments. When this happens, guide them toward the club you had in mind. Students will be working as clubs throughout this bend, so it's important that they are doing work that will move them forward as readers. Of course, in some ways, most of your students can't go wrong. The three major choices—literary language, fluency, and keeping track of the story—are very likely to be just what most of your students will need to practice—particularly students reading at or near the benchmark level for this time of year.

Divide large clubs into smaller ones.

Since there are three goal clubs, if your class divides evenly, you may find these groups to be very large. As you move from child to child, helping them to select goals, you might also keep a running list of which student has selected each goal. Then, near the end of reading time, you can take a moment to strategically create lists of three to four students for each club. For example, if eight students chose the fluency club, you may divide them into two groups of four, so it is easier for them to work together. We suggest making decisions about group membership based on reading levels as well as reading behaviors and interests.

MID-WORKSHOP TEACHING **Selecting a Goal**

"We are getting close to our first club meeting. Very soon, it will be time to choose your goal. Now is a good time to think about what you just read and to reflect on your reading. Ask yourself, 'Did I read that smoothly?' and 'Did I understand all the literary language?' and 'Am I clear about what is happening in the story?'

"Some of you may already know which goal club you want to join, and some of you may still be deciding. Either way, reflect right now on what you have done really well as a reader today, and what may need more work. When you know which club you want to join, jot down your name, plus your choice of goal club on a Post-it just like mine." I held up my own sample Post-it, where I had written my name, plus "Fluency" as my goal. "You'll have a few more minutes to decide, and then I'll be collecting these Post-its to set things up for your first club meeting."

SHARE

Launching Clubs

Channel children to meet under the chart for the skill focus area they would like to address.

"Ready to meet your new club members? I collected your Post-its and divided you into clubs with students who have the same goal as you. There are three or four of you in each club. Your Post-its with your names and goals are now on a new piece of paper with the names of all your club members. Find your name and sit with your new club members. The area where you meet today will become your clubhouse. It's time to find your club!" Students scattered about the room.

Give students tips for working in their clubs.

"You are now sitting with students who share your reading goal. Start by rereading the items on your club's chart. Then, think about how you can help each other with your goal. I've left a tip sheet for each club to help get you started. Feel free to add to it if you have other ideas."

Club Tip Sheets

Fluency Club Tip Sheet
- Read parts of your books out loud to each other.
- Practice using the strategies on the chart.
- Give each other feedback.

Literary Language Club Tip Sheet
- Share the literary language you found in your book.
- Discuss what the language could mean.
- Practice using the strategies on the chart.
- Help each other figure out the meaning.

Keeping Track of Longer Books Club Tip Sheet
- Retell your stories to each other.
- Practice using the strategies on the chart.
- Help each other understand what is happening in the story.

Before the share, take the goals students have chosen and use them to help you quickly organize kids into groups of approximately three or four students. For example, if seven students chose the literary language club, you may divide them into a group of three and a group of four. Make your decisions about how to group children based on reading levels, as well as reading behaviors, habits, and interests. Put the Post-its with club members' names and goals on one piece of paper per club, and place each of those on a table or the rug or another area where that club will meet regularly.

Session 15

Organizing Goal Clubs

MINILESSON

IN THIS SESSION, you'll teach readers that reading clubs need to create their own clear plans to accomplish their goals.

CONNECTION

Share an anecdote that highlights the importance of making a plan.

"Readers, my family and I recently started a new project at home. We decided to paint our bedrooms! Do you think we just grabbed a brush and started painting? No, way! First, we picked out some paint color samples. Then, we put little squares of the sample paint up on the wall and decided together which colors we were going to use. Then, we made sure we had all the tools we needed to help us do the job. We picked up paintbrushes and drop cloths and painter's tape. I think you get the idea," I said.

"I bet you're wondering what this has to do with reading clubs, right? Well, just like my family needed to have a plan and gather tools before we started to work, reading club members need to do that, too. Readers can make plans and gather up the tools they need to do the work of reading.

"Yesterday, I asked you to do something that is really challenging. Choosing a goal based on what you need to improve upon is challenging work, and you did it!" I said enthusiastically. "But when I listened in to your club meetings, I realized that you need a few tips to get your clubs up and running smoothly."

❖ **Name the teaching point.**

"Today I want to teach you that reading club members work together, sharing what they know with each other and making plans to reach their goals. You can gather tools around the room, make your own charts, and help each other make a plan so you're ready to work together toward your goals."

GETTING READY

- Display a list of questions for each group to consider when making a plan (see Teaching).

- Select a group of students with whom to model creating a club plan. We recommend you choose a group that needs extra support with this (see Teaching).

- Ask students to sit with their clubs on the rug and distribute a blank Club Plan to each group for recording their plans (see Active Engagement).

- Create a new anchor chart titled "Working Together in Goal Clubs" and prepare to add the strategy Post-its—"Create a plan." and "Talk together." (see Share).

SESSION 15: ORGANIZING GOAL CLUBS   97

TEACHING

Give students guiding questions to help them create their club plans.

"When my family and I sat down to make a plan, we first had to ask ourselves some questions." I held up my index finger and asked, "What do we want to accomplish?" I held up my next finger and said, "What will we need to do this?" I held up another finger and said, "What will happen first, then second, then third?" I then displayed this list of questions with the document camera.

> **ANCHOR CHART**
>
> **Working Together in Goal Clubs**
>
> Create a plan
> - Goal: What do we want to accomplish?
> - Tools & Materials: What will we need to do this?
> - Steps: What will happen first, then second, then third?

Model answering the questions with a club that needs more support, helping students create a reading club plan.

"Guess what, readers? You can ask yourselves these very same questions to guide your planning. Let's practice this. Can the literary language club of Maya, Philip, and Maddie stand up here with me? Pretend that I am a member of this club. Let's make a plan, using the questions to guide us."

I displayed the blank Club Plan with the document camera for students to see.

"First question: 'What do we want to accomplish?'" I said, and gestured for children in that club to answer.

"Well, that's easy," Maya said. "To understand the literary language in our books!"

"Great!" I said, writing the goal down on the Club Plan. "Okay, next question: 'What will we need to do this?'"

"We can use the chart," Philip said.

"Oh, let me write this down." I jotted "chart" on our Club Plan. "What else?" I asked the club.

"Maybe Post-its with literary language from our books?" Maddie suggested.

"Fantastic! Anything else?" I asked.

Club Plan

| Club Members: |
| Goal: |
| Tools: |
| Steps: |

FIG. 15–1 Sample reading club plan

As you listen to students, you might offer additional suggestions that build upon and extend their ideas. For example, if students suggest that they will need Post-its for jotting down literary language, you might add that they could create a large poster to collect all their literary language Post-its.

When no students responded, I suggested that in addition to their books, the club might also need some poems to share in case books didn't have much literary language, as well as a big poster to capture all the literary language they found. I jotted these ideas down on the Club Plan.

I posed the next question: "What will happen first, second, then third?" As club members made suggestions, I synthesized and recorded them on the Club Plan.

Club Plan

Goal: To understand literary language in books

Tools & Materials: Chart, Post-its, books, poems, pencils, large poster

Steps: First, one club member will share an example of literary language from his or her book. Second, that person can say what he or she thinks it might mean or ask a question about it. Third, other club members can say what they think it might mean or ask questions.

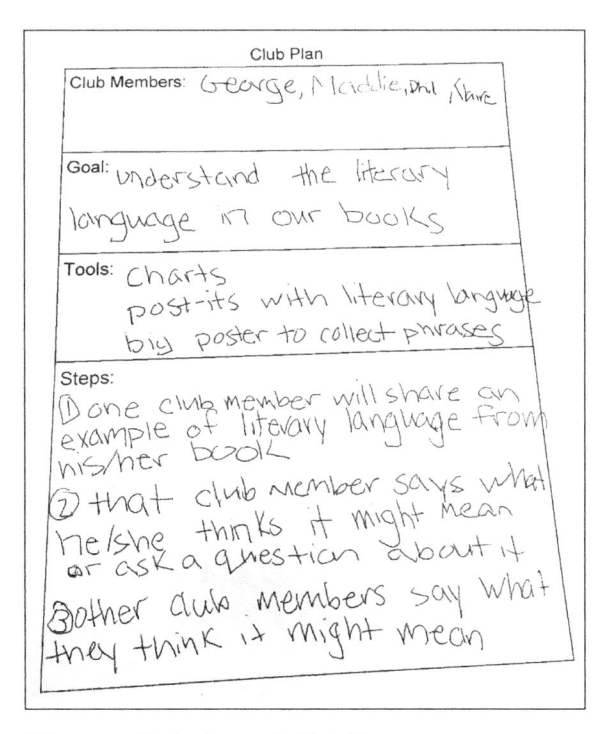

FIG. 15–2 Student sample Club Plan

ACTIVE ENGAGEMENT

Coach clubs as they create their reading club plans, supporting their work with questions, suggestions, prompts, and tools.

"I'm going to give each club a piece of paper that says 'Club Plan' at the top. Use this to write down your plans so you don't forget them." I passed out a blank Club Plan to each group.

"When I say go, turn and face your club members. Then answer the same guiding questions we used to create your own club plan. Once you have a draft, you can review it and add to it or make changes." I gave the literary language club their draft plan to review, revise, and extend. I said to the whole class, "Readers, are you ready? Go!"

As clubs made plans, I moved around to each group and coached their work. If students struggled to come up with ideas for tools to use, I made some suggestions: a large poster to collect special language for the Literary Language Club, a voice recorder for the Fluency Club, lots of Posts-its, and special bookmarks to note important events for the Keeping Track of Longer Books Club.

After a few minutes of coaching, I stopped the club planning. "Readers, you are coming up with some great plans! Make sure that everyone has a chance to share ideas. And don't forget to write down your plans to help you remember what you've agreed to do as a club."

After a few more minutes I stopped students and said, "Fantastic job, clubs! Now, when you meet, all you have to do is look at the plan you created together, and you'll know what to do."

LINK

Set students up to read independently, while thinking ahead about their clubs' activities.

"Today, when you are reading, think about what you can do to help prepare for your club meeting later today. The Fluency Club, for example, may be bringing a part to read aloud fluently to the group, since part of their routine is rereading parts of their books. Think about what you will need to do during independent reading today, so you are ready for your club meeting. When you know what you need to do to prepare for your reading club, give me a thumbs up, so I know you're ready for reading workshop."

Today's active engagement will be a little longer than usual, to provide time for clubs to create and write down a plan for their work together.

When students work in clubs, it is often helpful to establish some clear guidelines. For example, each club may have a special place to keep their club materials. It can be their "clubhouse." You may also choose to create specific roles for members of each club. For example, one student may be the timekeeper, one student may be in charge of supplies, and so on.

Some clubs may struggle to identify steps to take to help them reach their goals. Coach students to create a plan that involves all club members participating and talking. For example, the Keeping Track of Longer Books Club should give each club member a chance to retell, as well as time for questions.

CONFERRING AND SMALL-GROUP WORK

Using Shared Reading to Help Clubs Meet Their Goals

THIS IS A CONVENIENT TIME to meet with students to support them in mastery of their goals, as they are already sitting with students who have similar goals. Shared reading is a great tool to use when meeting with clubs, because it builds community with a shared text and encourages repeated readings. For example, you may choose a song or poem to read with the fluency club. As you sit with them you can practice scooping up words into phrases, finding the right tone of voice to use, and rereading until you find a just-right pace.

Then, you can use the same poem or a different one and meet with the literary language club. With this group, you can highlight literary phrases and help students discuss the meaning of them. You might leave copies of the poem with the group so they can keep working on it together.

The group that is focusing on keeping track of longer books can also benefit from shared reading. Perhaps as you read a chapter of a book together, the students might make a timeline of events to keep track of the story. You could leave the next chapter with them, so students can continue this work independently.

MID-WORKSHOP TEACHING **Preparing for Club Meetings**

"Readers, can I stop you for a minute? You have a bit of independent reading time left, and then it will be club time. One thing to keep in mind is that no matter what club you are in and what plan you made, you will be talking with your club members today. Whenever we get together with a group to talk, there are some things we can do to prepare. Remember to have something ready to say to your club members that will help the club work toward its goal. Maybe it's a question about a part of your book, or maybe it's a new strategy to practice. If you prepare something to share with your club now, then when club time comes, everybody will have something to contribute. Right now, jot down something you want to share with your club today. Okay, keep reading."

SHARE

Growing Our Talk to Help Reach Club Goals

"Readers, you already have a plan for meeting with your club, so you're almost ready to start. When you meet with your club, make sure that everyone gets a chance to talk, one at a time. Look at the person who is talking, and nod or comment to show you are listening. You are big second-graders now, so you don't need to raise your hand. Just let another club member finish before you start talking. You can ask questions about what another club member said. If another club member is not contributing, you can ask them what they think. And please remember to be polite. Clubs work so much better when everyone is polite."

I shared the beginning of our "Working Together in Goal Clubs" chart.

ANCHOR CHART

Working Together in Goal Clubs

- Create a plan
  - Goal: What do we want to accomplish?
  - Tools & Materials: What will we need to do this?
  - Steps: What will happen first, then second, then third?
- **Talk together**
  - Look at the person talking.
  - Nod at comments to show you are listening.
  - Ask a club member a question about what he or she said.
  - Ask students who are not contributing what they think.
  - Let another club member finish before you start talking.

I gave students a moment to review the chart silently.

Then I said, "So now that you're prepared for your club meetings, go ahead and get started!"

Session 16

Giving Feedback to Group Members

IN THIS SESSION, you'll teach children to support each other's work by giving helpful feedback.

MINILESSON

CONNECTION

Recruit children to work together and remind them of the upcoming grand celebration.

"Readers, once when I was on a picnic, all of a sudden I noticed there were ants everywhere. Before screaming or reacting, I took a second to watch them. They were carrying some of my sandwich crumbs back to their colony. Each ant was doing its part, and they were all working together. Thinking about that reminds me of you. No! I don't think you are ants. I do think, however, that you can work together and help each other meet your goals, just like the ants worked together to meet theirs.

"As you know, we are getting close to the end of our unit, and to our reading celebration when we will share our accomplishments with each other!" I pointed to the calendar on which I had circled the date of the celebration. "Before we celebrate, though, we still have a bit more work to do. I was thinking that I couldn't possibly get to every single one of you today, so I have a question for you. Do you think you could help each other—that you could teach each other today?"

"Yes!" the children chimed.

❖ Name the teaching point.

"Today I want to teach you that club members can give each other feedback to help one another meet goals. One way you can do this is by using the anchor chart to guide you. You can look to see what a club member is doing well and what he or she may need help doing."

GETTING READY

- ✓ Display a class calendar with a celebration date circled (see Connection).
- ✓ Coach one club to model giving feedback to each other (see Teaching and Active Engagement).
- ✓ Display the anchor chart from the first bend, "Making Your Reading More Fluent" (see Teaching and Active Engagement).
- ✓ Prepare to use a prop, such as a director's board, if available, for starting and ending a role-play (see Teaching and Active Engagement).
- ✓ Display the anchor chart "Working Together in Goal Clubs" so that it is ready to refer to, and prepare to add the strategy Post-it—"Help each other" (see Share).

TEACHING AND ACTIVE ENGAGEMENT

Assemble one reading club in a fishbowl to model giving effective feedback to each other, while the other children observe and note their behaviors.

"Readers, when I say 'Go,' could you please move your bodies and make an oval in the meeting area? Are you ready? Go!" I commended the children for quickly changing their positions. Then I said, "In a moment, we are going to ask one club to sit in the middle of the rug. We are creating a fishbowl. That means, we will sit on the outside watching what is happening in the middle. Your job, however, is not just to sit there and watch. Your job is bigger than that! When the club starts meeting, your job is to watch their every move and think about how they are working together to help each other improve their reading. What are they doing? What are they saying?" Then, I called the club that I had prepared to come into position in the middle of the fishbowl.

Next, I placed our fluency chart from the first bend on the easel so that the club members could use it while giving feedback.

During this minilesson, students engage in inquiry to study the behaviors and methods of a club that effectively gives feedback. They become active observers as they watch the club and reflect on their actions. You could easily tell the children what they should do; however, enabling students to discover it on their own is more engaging.

Asking students to study what the club is doing enables all the children to take an active role in the minilesson. The students who are looking into the fishbowl are analyzing the conversation to name its transferable qualities.

Then, I began to build the excitement as I pulled out my director's board and said, "When I say, 'Action,' the club will begin their work. Is everyone ready? Club members? Observers?" The students waited in anticipation. "*Action!*" I said as I clapped the board together.

In the fishbowl, Amelia asked, "Can I share first?" The other club members nodded in agreement. "Let's read the chart first to help us think about what we should be looking for," Daniel said. George began to point to the chart and read it aloud to the club. Then, Amelia began to read.

Emma said, "I like how you scooped up the words into phrases. I think you can practice your just-right pace. It sounded a little too fast. Why don't you try it again, Amelia?"

George said, "Let's keep our thumbs up when it sounds like just-right reading and move them sideways when it's too fast. That will tell you to slow down a bit. Okay?"

"Sounds good," said Amelia.

"Cut!" I said with another clap of the director's board. "Wow, think about how the club members really helped each other with their reading. Did they just say, 'Good job' to each other and move on? No way. Think about what they did and turn and tell your partner right now."

Listen in and restate the behaviors that children noticed into clear, transferable club behaviors.

I moved around the circle to listen in and coach several children. Then, I gathered students back to recap and create a list of ways that club members can help each other. I said, "I heard so many of you talking about what this club did that you could also try." I held up my first finger and said, "I heard some of you mention that they agreed who would go first." Lifting my second finger, I said, "Each club member really listened and used the chart to think about a compliment and something to practice." I lifted my third finger and said, "There was time for practice and a clear plan for how to help another club member."

LINK

"So readers, you'll have time to read independently today to enjoy your books and work on your reading goals. When it's time for clubs today, remember that you have a very grown-up, important job to do today. Your job is to really, really listen to your fellow club members, thinking about how you can help them meet their goals. Remember to use the chart to help you think of things to practice."

CONFERRING AND SMALL-GROUP WORK

Leading Goal-Oriented Strategy Groups

Give students additional ideas and support each club in meeting its goal.

Since each goal club is already organized by need, you have the perfect opportunity to lead several strategy lessons today, helping children work toward their goals. You can think about which strategies each group needs more practice with to meet its goal. The focus of your work will be different for each group. For example, if you are working with a fluency group, you may decide to teach them to record their reading so that they can replay it and listen to themselves. This could help children reflect on their oral reading. Then, you might teach them to record themselves again after they've practiced to reassess themselves.

If you are working with a literary language group, you may decide to teach them to use additional resources when solving literary language. You may, for example, teach children how to use a search engine, or an app, or another resource to find the meanings of idiomatic expressions. Yes, you could tell children what these expressions mean. However, it helps to give them strategies that will help them to be independent and able to carry on without you.

If you are working with a club focused on keeping track of longer books, you might coach students to use all the strategies they know for retelling. You may teach them to practice retelling by using the Post-its on which they had recorded important events. The goal clubs, like any book club or reading partnership, provide an authentic audience for retelling the stories children are reading and for engaging in meaningful conversation related to the text.

MID-WORKSHOP TEACHING
Giving Helpful (Specific) versus Unhelpful Feedback

"Readers, can I stop you for a second? I want to give you a little tip about feedback. Feedback and suggestions can be really helpful, or not so helpful. The more specific we are, the more helpful it usually is. Let me give you an example. I could say, 'I can't understand what you're reading.' But I could be more specific and say, 'Your voice is loud enough, but you're reading so quickly that it's hard to understand. Slowing down your pace a little would help.'" I pointed to the last bullet on the fluency chart. "Wouldn't that be more helpful?" Children nodded thoughtfully.

"If I suggest that you solve that tricky phrase, is that helpful? Maybe a little. What if I use the chart to help me find something more specific to say, like, 'Solve that tricky phrase by picturing both things being compared?' Isn't that *more* helpful?" I said. Students nodded in agreement. "Why?" I asked. They noted that it told the reader specifically what to do.

"Today when you are working in your club, remember to try to make your feedback and suggestions as helpful as possible. Helpful feedback is clear and specific about what's happening and what to do about it."

SHARE

Helping and Teaching Club Members to Reach Our Goals

Suggest that club members model suggestions for each other.

"Readers, in a moment you are going to meet with your fellow club members. You have been working toward your goals and thinking about how to help each other. Before I send you off today, I have one more tip for you. If you feel that another club member needs more help understanding what you are teaching, show them how you do it. That's what teachers do, and, as club members you are helping and teaching each other," I said. I added the final strategy to the anchor chart.

ANCHOR CHART

Working Together in Goal Clubs

- Create a plan
  - Goal: What do we want to accomplish?
  - Tools & Materials: What will we need to do this?
  - Steps: What will happen first, then second, then third?
- Talk together
  - Look at the person talking.
  - Nod at comments to show you are listening.
  - Ask a club member a question about what he or she said.
  - Ask students who are not contributing what they think.
  - Let another club member finish before you start talking.
- **Help each other**
  - **Give a compliment.**
  - **Give a tip.**
  - **Be specific.**
  - **Show how you do it.**

"Now it's time to put all you're learning into action with your clubs. Try today to really work on giving each other helpful feedback and guidance about what club members are doing well and what they might work on next. Off you go!"

SESSION 16: GIVING FEEDBACK TO GROUP MEMBERS

Session 17

Celebration

GETTING READY

- Display the anchor charts from all bends, including "Making Your Reading More Fluent," "Understanding Literary Language," and "Keeping Track of Longer Books" (see Connection). 👆
- Prepare to act as a researcher with glasses, clipboard, and pen (see Teaching).
- Ask students to come to the meeting area with a book to read (see Active Engagement).
- Display the goal club anchor chart, "Working Together in Goal Clubs" (see Link). 👆
- Give each goal club paper and markers to create a research bulletin (see Mid-Workshop Teaching).

MINILESSON

In the connection, begin by telling your students that today is a day for celebration. Show them the charts from each bend that illustrate everything they have learned during this unit. You might start by looking at the "Making Your Reading More Fluent" chart. Ask children to read the chart aloud, making sure to read it fluently. Then you might move to the "Understanding Literary Language" chart and invite children to give examples of some of the literary language they've encountered. Finally, direct children to the "Keeping Track of Longer Books" chart, perhaps asking them to recall a longer book they read and share key events in the story.

You might then set up your teaching point by saying, "You have been learning from research scientists throughout this unit about how to tackle these longer, harder books you're reading. I'm thinking that today, you can become the research scientists! As a goal club, you can create your own news bulletin and publish your findings about what readers need to do to tackle harder books. Are you up for it?"

Your teaching point could be, "Today I want to teach you that readers can be researchers. Readers can really study others in their clubs to notice what they do and how they do it. Then readers can publish their findings so others can learn from them."

In your teaching, you may teach students to study other readers, noticing what strategies and skills they are using. You may model this by having all students read on the rug. You can walk around pretending to be a researcher and put some glasses on, for effect. You can hold a clipboard and a pen and listen closely as students read, jotting down notes. Voice over to students how you jot down when readers reread or slow down or use expressive voices. You may tell students that researchers also ask questions to understand more about what's happening. Model asking questions, such as "What does that phrase mean?" or "How do you know that?" or "What happened in the story?" or "How do you remember that?" You might show the class your notes at the end, sharing the skills and strategies you noticed students using.

In the active engagement, you might announce to students that it is their turn to be researchers. Have one partner begin as reader and one partner begin as researcher. You may ask the researching partners to jot down skills and strategies they are noticing. Coach and voice over to encourage the researchers to ask questions. Then ask students to switch roles, so each has a turn as both researcher and reader.

In the link, you may emphasize that, as students read today, they can also research themselves as readers, noting what skills and strategies they are using. You may also remind students of goal club routines and procedures, as it is their last day to work together toward their club goals. You may remind children to refer to the anchor chart, "Working Together in Goal Clubs."

CONFERRING AND SMALL-GROUP WORK

As you confer with individual children and pull together small groups, move around the room and notice all the growth your students have made. You may look back at your conference notes from the beginning of the unit, and as you read with students today, try to note their progress. You can also be on the lookout for students who are ready to change book levels. You can make a list of students who may need to be reassessed at the start of the next unit.

In addition, you can support clubs in their creation of a research news bulletin. You can coach students to work collaboratively to create a news bulletin that reflects what they worked on as a club.

Breaking News About Second Grade Readers!

When you read longer books, using post-its at the end of each chapter can help you remember the whole book.

Breaking News About Second Grade Readers!

Did you know that 2nd graders can change the sound of their reading voices? YES, they can! Rereading out loud and practicing with partners can make their reading sound smooth and like a storyteller.

FIG. 17–1 Students release their own news bulletins to reflect on what they learned.

SESSION 17: CELEBRATION

109

Mid-Workshop Teaching

In your mid-workshop teaching, you may announce to students that they'll move into their clubs a bit early today. You might give each club a piece of paper and markers and announce that each club will create a news bulletin about their goal, now that they are experts on it. You can coach clubs to really show off what they have learned and practiced as a club in their bulletins.

SHARE

In the share, you may invite your readers to join you on the rug, sitting with their goal clubs. You might say to children, "You have done such powerful research that it's worth publishing. I'm thinking that we can share our research with other readers! Perhaps we can put the news bulletins you created in the school paper, or send them home as a memo, so all readers can know about your reading research and use it to help them become better readers." Then, you can have each club read their research news bulletin to the rest of the class. When your celebration is complete, collect the research students have done and publish it!

You might want to use writing workshop to have students revise and edit their research bulletins before publishing and distributing them.

Read-Aloud and Shared Reading

Read-Aloud

GETTING READY

✓ Choose a chapter book with an engaging storyline and rich language to use repeatedly throughout these sessions. We use *Minnie and Moo Go Dancing* by Denys Cazet.

✓ For Session 1, ask students to bring several Post-its, and a pencil to the meeting area. Prepare a piece of chart paper to model jotting down notes during the read-aloud.

✓ Prepare a piece of chart paper to list rules of accountable talk ("When talking about books . . .") and display it throughout the sessions.

✓ Display the accountable talk chart with prompts from the Unit 1 *Second-Grade Reading Growth Spurt* titled "Readers Talk about Books," so that students can refer to it for ideas during discussions.

✓ For Sessions 2 and 3, ask students to sit next to their reading partners. After reading, be ready to ask them to sit in a circle.

Getting Ready: BOOK SELECTION

Engaging, longer chapter books make good read-aloud choices for this unit. This way, you can model much of the work students will be doing, as many of their independent reading books are growing longer at this point in the year. By choosing a chapter book, you can support students' capacity to track a story across several days and build their stamina. We recommend choosing a chapter book that contains one long story, such as *Iris and Walter* by Elissa Haden Guest, *Mercy Watson* by Kate DiCamillo, or, as we have chosen, *Minnie and Moo Go Dancing* by Denys Cazet. These are preferable to chapter books in which each chapter is a different story, such as the Frog and Toad books by Arnold Lobel or the Poppelton books by Cynthia Rylant. This unit and read-aloud structure focus on helping students build a cumulative understanding of the entire story, so books with many shorter stories won't work as well to support those skills. However, in *Minnie and Moo Go Dancing* and chapter books that have one central plotline, readers must carry the story from chapter to chapter.

In selecting a book, it's also important to think about the presence of literary language, which is a big focus of the unit. The more interesting language and vocabulary you can expose students to, the better! This is another reason we chose the book *Minnie and Moo Go Dancing*, as it's chock-full of literary language.

Don't feel that you need only read longer chapter books while teaching this unit, however. Picture books will still be an important part of your read-aloud

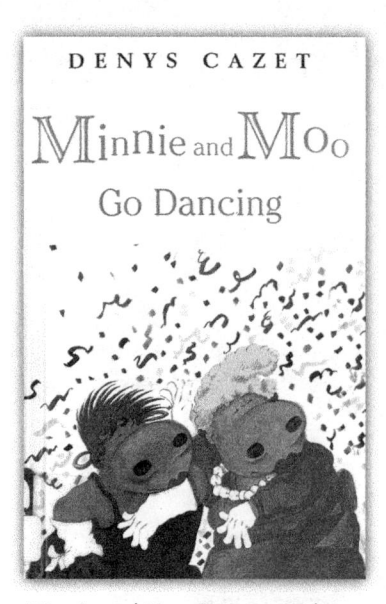

Minnie and Moo Go Dancing by Denys Cazet

repertoire. Students will also need to learn to keep track of what's happening in books that do not have chapters as a guide.

While this unit primarily focuses on fiction, you can still read aloud some nonfiction texts, of course. The first bend, which focuses on fluency, would be a great time to read aloud some nonfiction books so that students can transfer the skills they are learning to their reading of nonfiction. It would be a good opportunity to continue the work of the previous nonfiction unit of study to help students maintain and practice the skills learned in that unit as well.

In this unit, select texts for read-aloud at a range of levels. Choose some books above students' level, such as *My Name Is María Isabel* by Alma Flor Ada or *Iron Man* by Ted Hughes, which are both level O. Choose some read-aloud books, such as *Iris and Walter* by Elissa Haden Guest or *Minnie and Moo Go Dancing* by Denys Cazet, that are at benchmark levels (K/L), to model the skills that students currently need to work on independently. This read-aloud template will show you how to do the latter.

READ-ALOUD SESSIONS 1–5

GOALS/Rationale/Prelude

- We suggest that you read aloud *Minnie and Moo Go Dancing* (or an alternative of your choice) prior to Bend III. The book (or its alternate) is used quite a bit in that bend, and if students know the story prior to the minilessons that reference it, all the better.

- As you read the book aloud, invite students to engage with the text and practice strategies they have learned in previous units, such as taking a sneak peek and retelling, as well as those they are learning in the current unit. Think aloud to model comprehension strategies and prompt students to discuss tricky parts of the text with partners.

- As you read and discuss the book with students, highlight the unit's primary areas of focus, including fluency, literary language, and keeping track of story characters and events.

- Throughout these sessions, keep charts with accountable talk rules and prompts visible so that students can refer to them during their discussions.

SESSION 1

BEFORE YOU READ

Model how to preview a text, reading the title, studying the cover, and reading the back blurb.

"Readers, I'm so excited about this book we will read aloud together. It's called *Minnie and Moo Go Dancing* by Denys Cazet. Have some of you heard of these two characters? Wonderful! I thought, since we love to dance in here, this book would be so much fun for us to read together.

"Just like you do with your own books, let's start by taking a sneak peek at the cover and title." Hold up the cover or project it with the document camera, giving students a moment to take in the details. "Just by peeking at the cover, we're already learning some things about *these* friends." You might elicit a few observations from the class. "Yes, they are dancing cows in dresses. How silly!

"Let me flip to the back cover to check if there's a blurb that will give us a few more clues about the characters and the story. Oh, yes. Here it is. I'll read it to you. Will you think about the story and what might be the problem and its solution? Also, will you think about what kind of story this is?"

After students turn and talk, share a few responses. You might say, "Some of you said that maybe Minnie and Moo will find a way to go the farmer's party. Some of you said that maybe something bad will happen at the party, because Minnie and Moo are cows and they are serving hamburgers! I also heard some of you say this this story feels like it might be silly or funny. Let's read and find out what happens to Minnie and Moo."

After you have helped to set the class up to read, point out that there is no table of contents page in this book. Let students know that sometimes this happens. You can flip through to notice the chapter titles, even when there is no table of contents. Show students how to connect the chapter titles to the details gleaned from the blurb on the back of the book. You might say, "Today, we'll read the first three chapters: 'The First Wish,' 'The Second Wish,' and 'Magic.' The blurb on the back said, 'The farmer's house is lit up for a party. Gazing at it, Moo wonders why they can't be there, too. Why can't they go dancing?' Knowing the titles of the first two chapters, what do you think might happen in these first two chapters? Turn and talk."

AS YOU READ

Page 6: Pause and prompt students to use details from the text to figure out what's happening in the story.

The first few pages of this text can be tricky, as the reader needs to do lots of inferential thinking. To push students to do this inferential thinking, check that they are monitoring for meaning as well as paying attention to details in the text. You may ask, "What is Minnie doing here and *why*?" After the students turn and talk, you may decide to voice over, sharing a few examples of things children say, using words and details straight from the text.

Page 8: Pause and think aloud about which character is which, trying to keep the characters straight. Begin jotting down notes to model this strategy.

In *Minnie and Moo*, it is easy to confuse which character is Minnie and which one is Moo. You might say, "Wow, we are learning a lot about Minnie and Moo. Let's jot down some of what we are learning about these two characters." Draw a T-chart and think aloud as you begin to add to the chart, describing each character. The list can grow as you continue reading the book.

Minnie

- Appreciates the beauty of things (noticing the sunset)
- Blabs everything out

Moo

- Keeps thoughts and feeling inside

Pages 9–10: Guide students to use what they know about the characters and the book to predict what the character is thinking.

You may say, "As Moo looked at the farmer's house, what do you think she was thinking or feeling?" Encourage students to use what they know about Moo and the story, as well as the words the author uses in this part of the book, to infer what was on Moo's mind.

Page 11: Stop to help students notice the type of relationship the characters have.

"What type of relationship do the characters have? How do you know? Turn and talk." You may listen in and offer students prompts. You can prompt them to look at the T-chart created earlier with traits of the characters to guide them. Share some students' responses and add to them. Encourage students to notice that Minnie and Moo are great friends who try to make each other feel better when they are upset.

Page 13: Prompt students to jot down notes about the characters.

Continue adding to the T-chart started on page 8, asking students contribute to the list without your modeling. Since you have already modeled noticing characters' attributes, you may prompt students to notice the characters' dialogue or actions to add to the T-chart.

READ-ALOUD

Page 15: Teach students to stop and think about a piece of text and what it could mean.

Reread the sentence "'It's you!' said Minnie." Ask students to stop and think about what this phrase could mean. This is an example of the type of language students may not be used to, and pausing to stop, reread, and think about what it could mean will not only help them think about what's happening in the story, but also about how the author used special language to tell the reader something.

Page 18: Pause at the end of the chapter and think about the most important things that have happened in the story so far.

At the end of the chapter, you might ask students to think about what has happened so far in the story, and what is most important to remember as they keep reading. They'll later use Post-its to track the story, so pausing to think aloud or talk in partners at the end of this chapter will be good practice for both keeping track of the story and determining importance. You might say, "So many things happened in these first three chapters, as we were introduced to Minnie and Moo. Turn and tell your partner the biggest, most important things that happened—the things you'll want to remember as we continue reading." Reinforce that in this kind of longer chapter book, it will be important to keep track of what's happening in the story from one chapter to the next. In *Minnie and Moo Go Dancing*, the chapters are quite short, so we chose to do this at the end of chapter three. In longer books, you may decide to do this after each chapter.

AFTER YOU READ

Review whole-class discussion routines and prompt children to make book talk stronger.

Across the week, you will probably recruit the class to reflect on the read-aloud in several different ways. On this first day, you might engage the kids in a whole-class book talk. You might say, "We are going to have a book talk. You are becoming expert book talkers. What kinds of things do you do to have a *strong* book talk? Teach me!" You might create a quick list as children offer suggestions. For example, you might say, "These are wonderful things you should do *every* time you talk about books:

> When talking about books . . .
> - Look at the speaker.
> - Talk about THE BOOK.
> - Try to ADD on to what someone says.

"Let's talk about these three chapters and what we have learned about Minnie and Moo. Think about how these characters are similar and different and the type of relationship they have. Use your notes from the read-aloud. Remember to use the 'Readers Talk about Books' chart to keep the conversation going."

> **SESSION 1: AS YOU READ**
>
> **p. 18: Pause at the end of the chapter to think about the most important things that have happened in the story so far.**
>
> "So many things have happened in these first chapters. Turn and tell your partner the biggest, most important things that happened– the things you'll want to remember as we continue reading."

As students talk, you may prompt them to stay focused on the text and the prompt, making sure students are discussing the characters. Encourage them to refer to the "Readers TALK about Books" anchor chart to help them build upon their own and each other's ideas.

SESSIONS 2 AND 3

BEFORE YOU READ

Prompt students to list details they learned about the characters from the first three chapters.

"Readers, today we will read the next few chapters in *Minnie and Moo Go Dancing*. But first let's warm up our minds to get ready to read. We took a sneak peek before we started the book, but when you're continuing to read the same book, it helps to stop and retell what you know so far. You can say what you remember about Minnie and what you remember about Moo. Turn and tell your partner a list of things you know about Minnie. Say as many things as you can. Who is she? What does she do? What does she like and dislike? How does she act?"

Listen in, and then call on a few children to share their responses. "Now, talk about Moo. Go!" After a bit, share a few things that were said to help children remember the details. You might say, "So Minnie is the type of character who appreciates beauty. She is a bit bossy and blabs everything she thinks. Moo is a bit quieter. She wishes she could be more like people. They are both good friends to each other.

"We really learned *a lot* about these characters in just *three* chapters. As we read on, I bet we will learn even more. We might even be able to add new things to these lists!"

Flip through the pages to help students remember the story and the events that have happened so far.

"Let's get ourselves ready to read the next chapter. Let's reread the back cover again. Now let's review the titles of all the chapters we have read: 'The First Wish,' 'The Second Wish,' and 'Magic.' Let's flip through the pages we have read so far and think about what's happened. Turn and tell your partner what has happened so far." After students have shared, you can ask a partnership to share a retelling of the first three chapters.

Read the upcoming chapter titles to think about how the next part of the book might go.

You may say, "Let's look at the next few chapter titles and think about what might happen in those chapters." Read aloud the chapter titles: "The Party," "Doing the Moo," and "Hamburger." Ask students to discuss with their partners what they think the upcoming chapters might be about, prompting them to make predictions using the chapter titles, the back cover blurb, and what's happened so far in the story.

AS YOU READ

Page 21: Pause and think through the events together.

In texts at these levels, there are often jokes or silly bits that students may miss or struggle to understand. At these parts, you might stop and say, "Readers, this is so confusing. What just happened? Who just arrived? Let me reread and think about this." You might then reread page 21 and ask students to turn and talk about what just happened. After students have spoken to each other, gather them back to share. You might narrate, "So, when Minnie and Moo get to the party, everyone thinks they are Opal and Ruby, the farmer's sisters. They don't realize Minnie and Moo are cows! Their costumes fooled everyone."

Page 24: Ask students to stop and retell the important events of the chapter, trying to keep all the new characters straight.

This is a part where there are many new characters introduced, and a lot is happening. It's a good time to pause and say to readers, "Wow, so much just happened, and we met so many new characters. Stop and tell your partner all the new characters that appeared in this chapter and who they are."

Students may notice that Poopsie, Hank DePew, and Bobo DePew are all people at Farmer John's party. By stopping to think and talk with their partners, children can practice keeping track of all the characters and how they fit into the story so far.

Page 32: Provide students with some background knowledge and guide them in monitoring for meaning.

Students will need some background knowledge to understand why Minnie gasped and why the cows are so upset about eating hamburgers. You may need to explain to students what a hamburger is made of and remind them that Minnie and Moo are cows. You may say to students, "Why did Minnie gasp? Why did she tell Moo to put down the burger? Turn and talk." Point out to students that readers have to stop and think about these kinds of things, so they don't miss any part of the story.

Page 36: Encourage inferential thinking about events when a lot happens at once.

There are times in a text when many things happen at once. On page 36, students may be confused about all the recent events. You may ask students to turn and talk, asking, "Why are they worried about the Holsteins?" and "Who are the Holsteins?" You may say, "I am so confused. Let's reread these last few pages and make sure we understand all the events at the party." After students talk, you may bring them back together to make sure students understand the events. You may say, "Oh, so because Minnie and Moo ate the hamburgers, that are made from cows, they think they ate their cow friends, Bea and Madge Holstein. They run away, holding the burgers, saying 'I've got the Holsteins,' because they think the burgers are the Holsteins. Now I understand, because I slowed down to reread that part."

AFTER YOU READ

Ask students to sit in a circle. Guide them in doing a braided retelling of chapters 1 through 6.

At this point, after reading, you may say, "Readers, today we will do a braided retelling of all we have read so far in *Minnie and Moo Go Dancing*. We will sit in a circle, and one of you will start retelling from the very beginning of the story, just a bit. Then, each person will add a little bit more of the story, weaving in another strand. We will go around the circle until we have retold the events of chapters 1 through 6. Remember to listen to each other carefully and think about what detail or event from the story you will weave in when it is your turn." You might also remind students to use the names of characters and weave in words and phrases they remember from the book.

SESSION 4 (And Session 5, if Necessary)

BEFORE YOU READ

Flip through the pages to help students remember the story and the events that have happened so far.

"Let's get ourselves ready to read the next few chapters. Let's reread the back cover again. Now let's read the titles of all the chapters we have read: 'The First Wish,' 'The Second Wish,' 'Magic,' 'The Party,' 'Doing the Moo,' and 'Hamburger.'" Let's flip through the pages we've read so far and think about what has happened. Turn and tell your partner what has happened so far." After students have talked with their partners, you can ask a partnership to share a retelling of the first six chapters.

SESSION 2: AS YOU READ

p. 32: Provide students with some background knowledge and guide them in monitoring for meaning.

"Why did _____? Why did she tell _____ to _____? Turn and talk."

Read the upcoming chapter titles and think about how the next part of the book might go.

You may say, "Let's look at the next few chapter titles and think about what will happen in those chapters." Read aloud the chapter titles: "Ghosts" and "The Last Wish." Ask students to turn and talk about what the upcoming chapters might be about, prompting them to make predictions using the chapter titles, the back cover blurb, and what has happened so far in the story.

Set students up to listen to the final chapter with a specific focus.

You might say, "Think about all the things you have learned about the types of characters Minnie and Moo are. As we read the last chapters of this book, listen for more examples that prove they are best friends." Or, you might nudge children to consider the lesson the book aims to teach. You might say, "As I read, think about what important lesson you think Denys Cazet wants us to learn about friendship."

AS YOU READ

Page 38: Think aloud to model monitoring for meaning.

Again, you might stop and model thinking aloud, asking yourself questions about what is happening in the story. As students accumulate more and more of the story, it is important that they stop and check their understanding. You might pause, acting confused, and ask, "What's going on, why are they putting the marker on the grave? What are they thinking?" You might ask students to turn and talk, and then voice over, "Ohhh, so they think the hamburgers are the remains of Madge and Bea Holstein, and they want to bury them and put a marker on their grave."

Page 42: Invite students up to the front of the meeting area to act out a tricky part to foster comprehension of the text.

Sometimes when the text gets more complex and the story becomes harder to comprehend, acting out a part can help students understand what's happening. Ask four students to come up to the front of the classroom. Assign roles—one student as Minnie, one student as Moo, another student as Madge, and one as Bea. Reread pages 40–42, while students act out as you read aloud.

Page 48: Use the whole text to think about character traits.

You may bring students back to the T-chart started in Session 1. You may ask students to add to this chart, now that the book is finished. Remind students to use characters' actions and dialogue to help them add more details to the text.

Minnie

- Appreciates the beauty of things (noticing the sunset)
- Blabs everything out
- **Has ideas that get friends in trouble**
- **Likes to dress up**
- **Cares about not hurting others**

Moo

- Keeps thoughts and feeling inside
- **Wishes she were more like people**
- **Follows Minnie's ideas**
- **Likes to dress up**
- **Cares about not hurting others**

You may notice that some traits apply to both Moo and Minnie. For example, they both like to dress up. You could have students create a third column to their chart where they add traits shared by both Minnie and Moo.

AFTER YOU READ

Initiate a whole-class discussion about the message of the story.

"Let's think not just about this final chapter, but about the *whole* book and all the things these two friends have done together. Remember, authors often write with a lesson to their readers in mind. What important lesson do you think Denys Cazet wants us to learn about friendship? Put your thumb up when you have an idea."

Ask students to first turn and talk to their partners to discuss their ideas.

It can be helpful to ask students to first discuss their ideas with a partner before sharing their ideas with the whole class. This helps students gain confidence and get reassurance from their partners. Say to students, "Now turn and discuss with your partner what you think Denys Cazet wants us to learn about friendship." After a few moments, gather the students back together.

Initiate a whole-class conversation, reminding students of the rules and routines of accountable talk.

You might say to students, "In a moment, you'll begin to discuss what the author wants us to learn about friendship. Before you do, I want to remind you of a few rules to remember when we have a whole-class discussion. Remember, eyes on the speaker, one speaker at a time, no raising hands, and be polite! Also, remember to use the accountable talk moves chart to help our conversation." Make sure the chart is displayed so students can see it. Then, call on one child to begin the discussion. Encourage students to use pages from the book to support their ideas. As they are discussing the text, try not to intervene. You may decide to take notes and coach students as you circulate around the circle.

Summarize, provide closure to the conversation, and offer feedback.

When the conversation begins to dwindle, tell the students that three more speakers can talk, and then you'll close the conversation. You can provide closure to the conversation by summarizing the big, important ideas that students shared, complimenting them on something that you noticed—perhaps their use of a move from the chart—and offering them a tip to lift the level of their talk the next time.

SESSION 3: AFTER YOU READ

End: When the conversation dwindles, summarize, provide closure, and offer feedback.

"The big ideas that you shared were _____." Then say, "I would like to give you all a compliment. I liked how you _____. Next time we have a class conversation, you can work on _____."

Shared Reading

Text Selections

› *Happy Like Soccer* by Maribeth Boelts and illustrated by Lauren Castillo

› A familiar poem or song of your choice, for example "You Are My Sunshine" by Jimmie Davis and Charles Mitchell or the "Chicken Soup with Rice" poems by Maurice Sendak

Since books at these levels are often longer, we suggest using just a piece to reread each day for shared reading, perhaps just the first five pages. They are particularly rich in literary language, and a lot happens in them. It's a good idea to read the entire book to the class after you have done Day 1 of shared reading. Knowing the entire story will help them to do the retelling work, and to dig deep into the word-solving, vocabulary, and fluency work in the beginning days of the shared reading.

We chose this text for many reasons. It is written with beautiful poetic language, making it a great text to use to practice fluency. It is also bursting with great vocabulary and literary language that will support the work of the unit. *Happy Like Soccer* is a level M text, which is just a bit higher than the benchmark level at this point in the year. This makes it a great text to model with, as it is slightly higher than most students' reading levels. Another reason we chose *Happy Like Soccer* is its engaging story with dynamic characters and meaningful themes.

DAY ONE: Warm Up, Book Introduction, and MSV

The first day is dedicated to introducing the book to students and beginning to set the stage for all the work you will do within the unit. As you introduce the book, try to reinforce habits that you have taught in your previous units of study, such as setting yourself up to read using a sneak peek, using word-solving strategies, and retelling. Begin to draw students' awareness to skills that you will emphasize in this unit, such as reading fluently, noticing and understanding literary language and vocabulary, and tracking what's happening in the story.

Of course, shared reading of a new text also gives you the opportunity to work on some word-solving work. Select a few words to practice using higher-level word-solving skills, such as words with prefixes and suffixes. Together, you can practice finding the syllables, as in rid/ing and re/sched/uled, and have students practice trying both the long and short vowel sounds and figuring out which one sounds right.

WARM UP

Quickly introduce and read a poem or song to build excitement and help students get comfortable reading aloud. It could be a mentor poem from writing workshop or a song the class loves. We often use the song "You Are My Sunshine" written by Jimmie Davis and Charles Mitchell or the poem "Chicken Soup with Rice" written by Maurice Sendak (and sung by Carole King).

Children love reading and singing lyrics from favorite songs. You might choose a song, such as one from a popular recent movie, and say, "Readers, it's not only with books that we practice reading; it's with songs as well! Get your best singing voices ready!"

You might read and sing part of the song today, stopping midway through the song to say, "Wow! You sounded gorgeous! I loved how you tried to scoop up the words in each line as you sang it! I love how you matched your voice to the mood of the text!"

"Let's reread it one more time. Before you read, think about the story of this song. What is this song about?"

"Okay, with your partner, turn and talk about what the song is about." Give students a short time to discuss the song and then reread it one more time. Then say, "Now, let's read a brand-new book!"

DAY ONE FOCUS

- ✔ Warm Up
- ✔ Book Introduction
- ✔ Word Solving

GETTING READY

- ✔ Display a copy of a familiar poem or song to sing with students, perhaps using a document camera. We recommend the song "You Are My Sunshine" by Jimmie Davis and Charles Mitchell or the "Chicken Soup with Rice" poems by Maurice Sendak (see Warm Up).

- ✔ Prepare to share a familiar text a level or two above the reading level of most of your students. We suggest the first five pages of *Happy Like Soccer* by Maribeth Boelts (see Book Introduction and First Reading).

- ✔ Use a piece of paper to record students' predictions and keep inside the book (see Book Introduction and First Reading and After Reading).

- ✔ Display the word-solving anchor chart from the Unit 1 *Second-Grade Reading Growth Spurt*, "When Words Are Tricky, Roll Up Your Sleeves!" (see Book Introduction and First Reading).

- ✔ Choose three to five words from *Happy Like Soccer* to cover up. Choose words that will be tricky for students to decode, such as words with multiple parts, and words that require knowledge of what is happening to solve (see Book Introduction and First Reading).

BOOK INTRODUCTION AND FIRST READING

Give readers an introduction that builds excitement for the story and reinforces the book-previewing skill of taking a sneak peek that they learned in the first unit of study.

"Readers, let's take a look at the book we are about to read using all we remember about taking a sneak peek." Show the cover with the document camera. "Hmm, . . . Let's study this cover to get our minds ready. The title is *Happy Like Soccer*, and it's written by Maribeth Boelts and illustrated by Lauren Castillo. Do we know any other books by this author or illustrator?" Some students may know the book *Those Shoes*, also written by Maribeth Boelts. If students do know this book, you can make connections about what that story was about and how this one might be similar.

"Remember that it's also important to read the back blurb. Let's read it together." Read the back blurb to your class and have students turn and talk about what they think will happen in the story.

"I hear many of you talking about how Sierra loves soccer and wondering what will happen to her when she is playing soccer in this book. Be sure to use the title, cover, and back blurb to predict what the problem and solutions may be in this book." As students talked, I coached partnerships.

"Eyes back up here. So many great predictions, readers! Let's record some of our class predictions on this piece of paper and keep it in the book. When we continue to read, we can come back to these predictions to confirm or revise them." I listened and jotted notes as the class shared some predictions.

Predictions about *Happy Like Soccer*:

- The problem will be her aunt can't go to her soccer game.
- The problem will be nobody can come to her soccer game.
- Her problem is solved when her aunt comes to the game.
- Sierra will love soccer and win the big game.

Choral read the first five pages with students, using pace, prosody, and phrasing to showcase fluency.

Begin chorally reading the first five pages, using tons of excitement and expression. Encourage more and more students to read along with you by saying things like, "I hear voices scooping up words, and I hear great expression from so many readers," or "Let's reread this part to match our voices to what is happening in the text."

Review word-solving strategies from earlier in the year by covering up three to five words and asking students to use known strategies to solve them.

Make sure you have displayed the word-solving chart from Unit 1 where students can see it. Choose three to five words from the text to cover up. Choose words that will be tricky for students to decode, such as words with multiple parts and words that require knowledge of what is happening to solve.

Remind students of the word-solving strategies they know to help them solve the covered words. First, coach students to use meaning and syntax. When the word is covered, they may list a few possibilities of what it could be. Celebrate when students guess words that make sense with the story and words that are syntactically correct, even when guesses may be inaccurate.

You may choose to cover up the word *apartment* on page 1. If, at first, students guess *house* or *home*, applaud these guesses, as students are using meaning and syntax appropriately. Point to the chart to name the strategies they are using. When you uncover the word, point to and read the strategies: "Look through the *whole* word, part by part" and "Look for a word inside a word." Students may continue to try to solve the word until they get *apartment*. After students solve the word, reread the sentence again with a smooth voice.

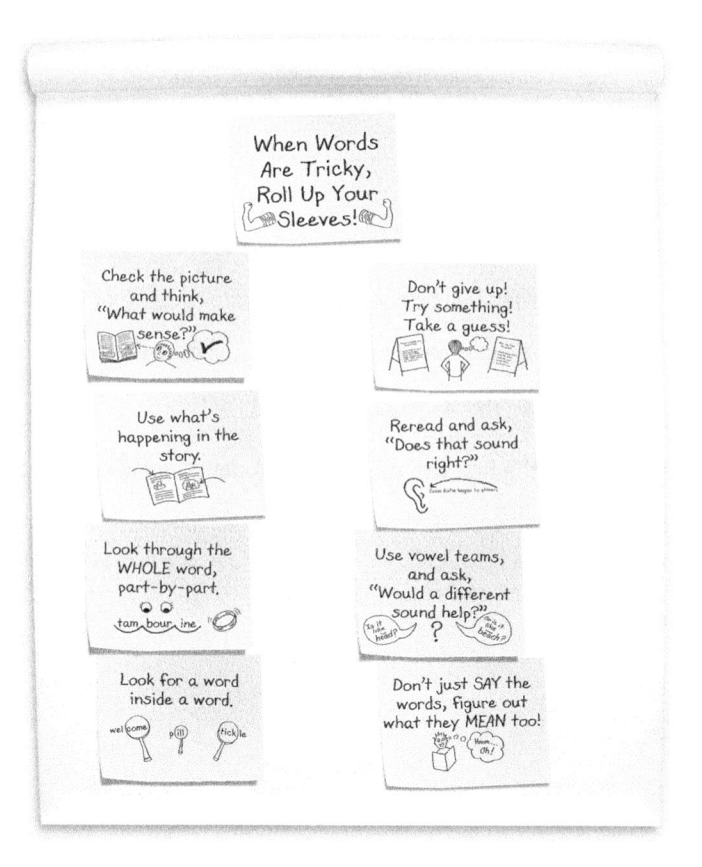

126   SHARED READING

AFTER READING

Review and update students' predictions.

Remind students of the importance of rereading. Not only is it important to make your voice smooth, but also to understand the story and track what's happening, so you can retell it from the beginning.

"Wow, so much has happened in this first part of the book. Let's reread our predictions and see if any were right, and if we need to add any more to this list." Coach students, who may notice that they were right in predicting that the big problem would be Sierra's aunt not being able to come to the soccer game. Some students may want to add predictions to the list, such as, "Sierra will make new friends on the soccer team." When you read the rest of the text during read-aloud time, students may continue to add to and revise their predictions.

Encourage discussions among partners, in which students reflect on their original predictions and add to and revise them, based on new information they have read.

Partners work together to retell what has happened so far with lots of details.

Remind students to retell the story, including important events and characters' feelings. Coach partnerships to use the title, back blurb, and what they know from the text to help them retell the story.

DAY TWO: Word Work

Day Two starts with rereading a familiar poem or song, such as the one used on Day One. Then you'll reread the first five pages of *Happy Like Soccer* and solve for tricky words. Students will have likely mastered basic decoding skills needed for this level of text; however, they'll need support in using more complex strategies. For example, students can practice trying the short vowel sound, and then the long vowel sound, to see which one sounds right, and then reading the word to check that it makes sense. Students may also need support using word parts such as prefixes and suffixes to solve words. With all of these more sophisticated word-solving strategies, it is important to remind students to use meaning and syntax when solving for tricky words as well. After solving each tricky word today, remind students to go back and reread the sentence again with the correct word to improve both fluency and comprehension.

WARM UP

Reread the song or poem from yesterday. If you chose a part of a long song or poem, such as "Chicken Soup with Rice," you may reveal more verses today. You can practice covering words in the song or poem to warm students up to word solve later in the book. When choosing words in the song to cover, choose words the K/L readers may stumble on, such as multisyllabic words or words that break conventional spelling rules or have undecodable chunks such as *tion*. When you cover these words, or use highlighter tape to pop them out, model effective word-solving behaviors. For example, at points of difficulty, model sliding your finger under the word as children check through all the parts. Then model rereading the entire sentence once the word is solved.

SECOND READING

Remind students of the word-solving strategies they know, add strategies to students' word-solving repertoire, and practice them with *Happy Like Soccer*.

Remind students of the first five pages of the book they read yesterday. You may say, "Let's take a picture walk through the first part of this book, which we read yesterday, and remind ourselves what was happening. Oh, remember that Sierra is on a new soccer team." Then turn the page. "Oh, remember this part when her aunt couldn't come, and it made her feel 'low around the edges.' Then she goes on the trip to the soccer game, and then she is playing soccer."

Today you'll reread the first five pages together. You may choose to go on to page 6, as it's full of longer multisyllabic words, which are great for practicing word solving. Prepare to compliment and prompt the work children do as they stop to tackle tricky words. You might drop your voice as children read aloud, listening for words readers do not recognize with automaticity. Prompt readers by saying, "You might know this word, but you might not! What can we do to figure this out?" To keep language consistent and build independence, nudge partnerships to look at the chart you developed during the first unit and apply these known strategies to figure out tricky words.

DAY TWO FOCUS

✓ Practice trying the long and then the short vowel sound to solve a word.

✓ Use syllables to solve words.

✓ Use prefixes and suffixes to solve words.

GETTING READY

✓ Project the text of a familiar song or poem from Day One (see Warm Up).

✓ Cover or use highlighting tape to highlight a few words in the song or poem. Choose words the K/L readers may stumble on, such as multisyllabic words or words that break conventional spelling rules or have undecodable parts, such as *tion* (see Warm Up).

✓ Prepare to share the next few pages of the text. We suggest the next three pages of *Happy Like Soccer* by Maribeth Boelts (see Second Reading).

✓ Display the anchor chart from Unit 1 *Second-Grade Reading Growth Spurt*, "When Words Are Tricky, Roll Up Your Sleeves!" so it is ready to refer to (see Second Reading).

128   SHARED READING

> **ANCHOR CHART**
>
> When Words Are Tricky,
> Roll Up Your Sleeves!
>
> - Check the picture, and think, "What would make sense?"
> - Use what's happening in the story.
> - Look at the first letters.
> - Look at the last letters.
> - Look through the *whole* word, part by part.
> - Look for a word inside a word.
> - Don't give up! Try something! Take a guess!
> - Reread.
> - Use vowel terms.
> - Figure out what the words MEAN!

You might stop on the word "uniform" and say, "This is a tricky one! Let's roll up our sleeves! What can we do? 'They cheer for me by the number on my _____, not knowing my name.' What is happening here?" Give kids a moment to mull over the possibilities before moving forward: "Some of you think it says *uniform*." As you move through the strategies, referencing the chart, prompt students to stop occasionally, using the three cueing systems to cross-check the word. Say, "Wait, did that word make sense, sound right, and look right? Let's check it!" Readers at levels K/L especially will need opportunities to practice solving multisyllabic words. You might pause on words, such as *neighborhood*, *restaurant*, and *remember*. With long words like these, readers will have to break up the word and then check to be sure it looks right, sounds right, and makes sense in the story.

At times, you may check even when words are read correctly. For example, you might read, "After the game, we ride back home, into the city, through my neighborhood." Stopping on *neighborhood*, you could say,

SHARED READING

"How do we know that is the word: *neighborhood*? Does that make sense? Does that sound right? Does that look right? Let's be absolutely sure!" At other times, you may intentionally read a word incorrectly and ask students to check it with you. For example, you might cover all but the *r* in the word *restaurant*, and you might say, "'. . . and right to the *room*.' That makes sense. Let's look through the *whole* word, part by part, to be sure." Revealing the rest of the word, you might say, "This word ends with *t*, but there's no *t* in *room*. So the word can't be *room*! What would make sense, sound right, *and* look right?"

Try to help students develop the habit of checking whenever they are unsure of a word. Sometimes they'll be right, and sometimes they won't. You might say, "Readers, since this is a tricky word, let's check it!" Always follow this up with, "Were you right? How do you know?" It's useful to have children name the strategies they use to solve words. "Point to the part of the chart that helped you!" you might say. Asking children to think about which strategies they are using can build their metacognitive skills and, ultimately, extend their independence.

AFTER READING

Practice using prefixes and suffixes to solve words.

You might let students know that, in this book, you have noticed lots of words with prefixes and suffixes. You may have students use their white boards and try adding a prefix or suffix to change the meaning to practice decoding these types of words. You may say, "Write the word *read* on your board. Now, change the word *read* to mean *read again*. Do this by adding just a few letters to the beginning or the end of the word." Coach students as they turn *read* to *reread*. "Wow, you're really getting the hang of this. Many of you knew to add the prefix *re* to the front of the word, and now you have made the word *reread*." You can practice a few examples with students on the white board and then transfer the work to *Happy Like Soccer*. You can reread sentences that have prefixes and suffixes and let students know that when they come to these words, they can use the prefix and/or suffix to help them decode the word and think about its meaning. You might highlight words such as *spying* and *rescheduled*.

Some prefixes and suffixes to look for in shared reading texts include the following:

Prefixes

un- means not

re- means again

dis- means the opposite of

im- means not

Suffixes

-less means without

-tion means the act of

-ing means doing

DAY THREE: Vocabulary and Literary Language

On the third day, you might reread the first five pages again, focusing on noticing literary language in the text.

WARM UP

Revisit the same song or poem you have been using, rereading the lyrics, each time building automaticity, fluency, and comprehension. Compliment students' efforts to reread and practice, supporting both confidence and engagement. Since the focus today is on literary language, consider highlighting some words or phrases that children might be unfamiliar with or that are key to understanding the text. Stop at phrases and think about what the author could have meant. Prompt readers to consider how the phrase contributes to the mood of the song. Then, reread the line in a voice that reflects an understanding of the words.

THIRD READING

Study literary phrases to determine the author's intent.

As you reread the first five pages of *Happy Like Soccer* today, plan to stop at literary phrases and discuss their possible meaning with students. You may model this a few times, on the first page or two. Then keep reading, asking students to take on the job of noticing literary language. You may stop at the phrase "shiny girls" and put some highlighter tape over this phrase. Ask students what they think the phrase means and why the author used it. Prompt students to notice that this is a new soccer team for Sierra and that "shiny girls" may be Maribeth Boelts's way of showing us that Sierra doesn't know these girls very well. You might talk about the excitement of having shiny new shoes that haven't been worn yet. Maybe she's pointing to the excitement of having new girls to play soccer with on a selective team.

Remind students of the strategies they know for paying attention to special language.

As you continue to read, stopping and noticing literary language, you can remind students to think, "What special meaning does the author want me to get?"

Keep reading, and ask students to put their thumbs up when they hear literary language. Some students may put their thumbs up when you read "my shoes have flames." Ask students to turn and talk about what the author could mean by that. Coach students to understand that Sierra's shoes don't actually have flames, but Maribeth Boelts is trying to show that she is running very fast.

DAY THREE FOCUS

✔ Use strategies to solve vocabulary words.
✔ Notice and solve similes.
✔ Notice and solve imagery.
✔ Notice and solve metaphors.

GETTING READY

✔ Display the familiar song or poem from Day One and Day Two. Highlight some literary language that children might be unfamiliar with or that is key to understanding the text (see Warm Up).

✔ Prepare to reread the same section of text you have shared the past couple of days. We suggest rereading the first few pages of *Happy Like Soccer* by Maribeth Boelts. Choose a few literary phrases to discuss with students (see Third Reading).

✔ Display the chart from Bend II, "Understanding Literary Language," so it is ready to refer to (see Third Reading).

SHARED READING

131

Notice many types of literary language.

Some students may notice that not only does the author use comparisons, but some of her words just create a special image. As you read, students may put their thumbs up at the part where it says, "low around the edges." Point out that this phrase is not typically used to describe a feeling. Remind students to reread that part and remember what is going on in the story. Prompt students to think about how Sierra must feel, knowing that she loves her auntie, who couldn't come to the soccer game because she had to work. Coach students to use clues in the phrase, such as the word *low*, to help them understand that it means Sierra is feeling sad.

AFTER READING

Retell parts of the text, incorporating literary language to demonstrate a larger understanding of the book.

After today's reading, you'll have many phrases highlighted in the text. Ask students to retell the story, trying to use as many phrases from the text as they can. For example, they might say:

> In the book *Happy Like Soccer*, Sierra joins a new soccer team, with new *shiny girls*.
>
> She is a very good soccer player and so fast that it is like her *shoes have flames*.
>
> The problem is that her auntie works on Saturdays and can't come to her games.
>
> This makes Sierra feel *low around the edges*.

Retelling the story using literary language helps students not only understand the literary language better, but understand the story better as well.

Practice using literary language in other contexts to promote transfer.

Let students know that this type of literary language can be used anywhere. You may give them an example such as, "Last night my brother was going to come over for dinner, and I cooked his favorite meal. He called me and told me he was sick just an hour before he was going to arrive. This made me feel *low around the edges*." Ask students to try to use examples of literary language from the book in other contexts to help them deepen their understanding.

DAY FOUR: Fluency

The fourth reading will focus on helping readers become increasingly fluent. Aim to focus on developing readers' pace, parsing, and prosody. Prosody involves making sure the text sounds right, with appropriate rhythm, stress, and intonation. Help your students listen to their own reading to check that it makes sense and sounds right with regard to phrasing, intonation, and stress on certain words or phrases. On this day, start by rereading the first five pages, and then you may choose to read a bit further in the text to give students more practice and to continue with the story.

DAY FOUR FOCUS

✔ Practice scooping up words into phrases.

✔ Practice reading at a just-right pace.

✔ Practice noticing the mood to read with expression.

GETTING READY

✔ Project the same familiar song or poem (see Warm Up).

✔ Display the anchor chart from Bend I, "Making Your Reading More Fluent," so that it is ready to refer to (see Warm Up and Fourth Reading).

✔ Prepare to reread the same section of text you have shared the past couple of days. We suggest rereading the first five pages of *Happy Like Soccer* by Maribeth Boelts (see Fourth Reading).

WARM UP

Reread the same song or poem again, explaining how accuracy, fluency, and comprehension improve with each read. Prompt readers to scoop up more words, noticing how line breaks and/or punctuation help guide the reader. Encourage readers to think about the mood of the song, paying attention to literary language and what's happening. You might divide the song into parts across partnerships so that Partners A and B are reading different lines, reciting the song in two voices. Invite kids to choreograph some movements and use facial expressions to bring the song to life.

FOURTH READING

Remind students of all they know about reading fluently by rereading the chart from Bend I.

As you begin rereading the first five pages of *Happy Like Soccer*, remind students that reading aloud can help fluency, so shared reading is a perfect time to practice all those strategies that improve fluency.

Emphasize using punctuation to scoop up words into phrases.

As you reread from the beginning, notice punctuation. There's a lot of punctuation on the first page of the text, so that might be a good place for students to practice using punctuation to help them scoop up words into phrases. They may practice rereading the same parts with different phrasing to figure out what sounds best. You might point out how commas help to guide the reader. Read, "My shoes have flames and my ball spins on this spread-out sea of grass with no weeds," in one scoop before pausing and reading in another scoop, "fields with no holes." Transfer this idea to the following pages where commas continue to support phrasing.

Ask children to do some interpretation work and think about the tone of voice that they should use when reading.

To support intonation, ask readers to think about what is happening in the text. For example, when you read the part where everyone has someone at the soccer game but Sierra, guide readers to think about which tone of voice to use

SHARED READING

133

when reading that part. You might prompt them by asking, "Will you read this part in a happy tone of voice? Or in a sad tone of voice?"

AFTER READING

Act out part of the story to deepen understanding.

The first part of the story is rich with characters and feeling. Characters include Sierra, the girls on her team, her auntie, and Coach Marco. You might break students up into groups of five or six and have each choose a role. Then you can reread the pages, as students act out scenes in their groups. This can help students deepen their understanding of this part of the book. Coach students to make their voices match how the characters are feeling and acting.

DAY FIVE: Putting It All Together to Understand the Story

Celebrate the work students have done reading and rereading the text, allowing the class to lead this final read, orchestrating all they have learned across the week. Be sure to have finished the text prior to this day. During shared reading, you may have only read through the first five to eight pages, but you should have finished the rest of the story during read-aloud or at another time in your day, so students know what happened in the story and can practice retelling it today. Then, consider ways you might extend the text, leading the class in a whole-group discussion, sharing questions or responses to the text, or perhaps even engaging in shared writing to compose a review.

WARM UP

Reread the now familiar song or poem for the final time with minimal teacher support.

Ask students to reread the same familiar song or poem with minimal teacher support. Allow students' voices to carry the reading. If some students still struggle with some of the words, other students will lead and help them. Try to sing the song or recite the poem in different ways, perhaps using a different voice. You might say, "Let's sing it again, pretending we are witches," or "Let's sing it again, pretending we are old grandpas!" Rereading in fun ways keeps rereading exciting, while building fluency.

DAY FIVE FOCUS

- ✓ Put all the skills of the week together.
- ✓ Retell the book and all the events in it.

GETTING READY

- ✓ Display the same familiar song or poem from the week of shared reading (see Warm Up).
- ✓ Display all the anchor charts you have referenced over the past few days, including "When Words Are Tricky, Roll Up Your Sleeves!," "Making Your Reading More Fluent," and "Understanding Literary Language" (see Final Reading).
- ✓ Prepare to reread the entire section of text you have been using for shared reading. Here we use the first five pages of *Happy Like Soccer* (see Final Reading).
- ✓ Use a blank piece of chart paper (or a projected page) for interactive writing of a review of the shared reading text (see After Reading).

FINAL READING

Emphasize how rereading can improve word solving and fluency, as well as bringing to light more literary language, which can help to improve understanding.

During your final reading of this text, ask your students to practice everything they have tried this week. Remind students, "As you read through the section you have been reading all week, you may stop to reread a part to smooth it out, or notice literary language you didn't recognize before. You might stumble over a word or two, but think about how you can reread it and use all the strategies you know to fix up your reading."

AFTER READING

Guide children to do a braided retelling of the entire book from the beginning, using the pictures and rereading for support.

While the shared reading has focused on the first few pages, you can reinforce readers' comprehension by asking children do a braided retelling of the story, in which one student starts the retelling, and then each student adds a bit more. Students can retell in this way as a whole class, or with their reading partners, or in a cluster of partnerships. One student may begin by saying, "Sierra is on a new soccer team," and then the next student might chime in, saying, "She loves playing soccer with her new team." The next one might add, "But the games are on Saturdays, and her auntie can't come because she works," and so on. By Day Five, students should have a strong understanding of the text, since many rereadings should have helped to build their comprehension.

Write a book review through shared writing, thinking about all that the author did in the text.

You might choose to extend the shared reading through shared writing. Together, the class might write a review of *Happy Like Soccer*. Discussing and writing about what the author did in the text can reinforce students' noticing and naming of the literacy language in the book. Talking and writing about these examples of literary language not only extends their comprehension of the story and the literary language used, but it can also push students' thinking about why an author would choose to write in certain ways, and what she wants her readers to get from the special language. Encourage children to think not only as readers, but as writers, too.

Credit lines continued from page ii

From *The Snow Day,* by Ezra Jack Keats, copyright © 1962 by Ezra Jack Keats; copyright renewed © 1990 by Martin Pope, Executor. Used by permission of Viking Books, an imprint of Penguin Publishing Group, a division of Penguin Random House LLC.

Minnie and Moo Go Dancing, by Denys Cazet. DK Publishing, 2000. Used by permission.

Materials by Kaeden Books and Lee & Low Books, appearing throughout the primary Reading Units of Study series, are reproduced by generous permission of the publishers. A detailed list of credits is available in the Grade 2 online resources.